Life, Death, and The Law

Landmark Right-To-Die Decisions

Maureen Harrison & Steve Gilbert
Editors

EXCELLENT BOOKS
SAN DIEGO, CALIFORNIA

Life, death, and the law

San Diego, CA 92192-7105

Publisher's Cataloging-in-Publication Data

Life, Death, and the Law: Landmark Right-To-Die Decisions/
Maureen Harrison, Steve Gilbert, editors.
  p. cm.
Bibliography:p.
Includes Index.
1. Right-to-die. 2. Terminally ill. 3. Assisted Suicide. 4. United States Supreme Court. 5. New Jersey Supreme Court.
I. Title. II. Harrison, Maureen. III. Gilbert, Steve.

R726.H24 1997   LC 97-60186
179.'7-dc20
ISBN 1-880780-13-5

In The Shadow Of Death

We are living longer. In 1950 Americans had a life expectancy of 68 years and 2 months. By 1995 that life expectancy had increased 11 percent to 75 years and 8 months.[1]

And dying slower. As a result of medical advances almost 90 percent of all Americans now die after a long illness.[2]

Our deaths have many causes. Some of the annual leading causes of death in America are: heart disease, killing almost 740,000; cancer, killing almost 540,000; stroke, killing over 150,000; lung disease, killing over 100,000; diabetes, killing almost 60,000; and AIDS, killing over 40,000.[3]

We may die in great pain. As many as 10 percent of all terminally ill patients require massive amounts of narcotics to relieve their unmanageable pain.[4]

And extreme mental anguish. Over 60 percent of all terminally ill cancer patients suffer severe psychiatric problems.[5]

Far from away home. Over 80 percent of all Americans die in a institutional setting - a hospital, hospice, or nursing home.[6]

An unknown number of terminally ill persons will commit suicide. Every year about 30,000 Americans, including an unknown number of terminally ill persons, commit suicide.[7] The suicide rate for New York City AIDS patients is reported to be 66 times higher than that of the general population.[8]

Suicide it is not illegal. No state currently has a law making either suicide or attempted suicide illegal.[9]

An unknown number of terminally ill persons will ask a doctor to let them die. An estimated 70 percent of the terminally ill die in an institutional setting after either refusing or withdrawing life-sustaining medical treatment.[10]

Refusing or withdrawing life sustaining medical treatment is not illegal. Beginning with 1976's *Karen Ann Quinlan* case, the courts have repeatedly recognized the right of the terminally ill to refuse or withdraw life-sustaining medical treatment.

An unknown number of terminally ill persons will ask a doctor to help them die. An estimated 25 percent of doctors have been asked by a terminally ill patient to help them die.[11] As few as 10 percent[12] to as many as 50 percent[13] of doctors (depending on their practice) admit to assisting terminally ill patients in committing suicide.

Physician-assisted suicide is illegal. The majority of states have laws criminalizing the act of assisting suicide.[14]

Laws banning physician-assisted suicide are under challenge. In 1994 the physician-assisted suicide laws of Washington and New York were challenged in Federal Court and declared unconstitutional. The U.S. Supreme Court agreed to definitively decide on the right of the terminally ill to commit physician-assisted suicide. That decision came down June 26, 1997.

Life, Death, and the Law presents, in plain English, the legal history and text of the landmark right-to-die decisions. In Section 1 you will find the New Jersey Supreme Court's *Quinlan* decision in the 1976 landmark case which established the first-ever state-wide right to refuse or withdraw life-sustaining medical treatment. In Section 2 you will find the United States Supreme Court's *Cruzan* decision in the 1990 landmark case which established the first-ever federal right to refuse or withdraw life-sustaining treatment. In Section 3 you will find the Ninth Federal Circuit Court's three *Compassion* decisions in the highly controversial

Washington State case, which declared in 1994 a federal right to physician-assisted suicide based on the Constitution's Due Process Clause. In Section 4 you will find the Second Federal Circuit Court's two *Quill* decisions in the equally controversial New York case which found in 1996 a right to physician-assisted suicide based on the Constitution's Equal Protection Clause. In Section 5 you will find the U.S. Supreme Court's final determination of these two right-to-physician-assisted-suicide cases in their 1997 landmark decision in *Glucksberg* and *Quill.*

Each of the right-to-die decisions presented in *Life, Death, and the Law* are carefully edited into plain-English versions of the original legal texts. Judge Learned Hand once wrote: *The language of the law must not be foreign to the ears of those who are to obey it.* The editors have made every effort to make the language of these decisions less "foreign." We have replaced esoteric legalese with plain English. Edited out are long alpha-numeric legal citations and wordy wrangles over abstract points of procedure. Edited in are definitions (standing = the right of a party to participate in a litigation), translations (certiorari = the decision of the Court to review a case), identifications (Appellant = Timothy Quill, M.D., Appellee = Dennis Vacco, New York State Attorney General), and explanations (who the parties were, what laws were at issue, what constitutional issues were involved, where the case originated, how the case reached the court, and what the final decision was). Preceding each edited decision we provide a history of the case and we note where the unedited decision can be found. The bibliography provides a selected list of further readings on the right to die.

Americans have many rights. *Life, Death, and the Law* is about their last rights.

M.H. & S.G.

Footnotes

[1]United States. Department of Health and Human Services. National Center for Health Statistics.

[2]United States. Court of Appeals, Ninth Circuit. *Compassion In Dying v. Washington State.* 79 Federal Reporter 3d (1996).

[3]United States. Department of Health and Human Services. National Center for Health Statistics.

[4]Humphry, Derek. *Dying With Dignity.* New York, NY: Carol Publishing, 1992, p. 33.

[5]Foley, Kathleen, M.D. *Competent Care For The Dying.* The New England Journal Of Medicine, Volume 336, No. 1 (January 2, 1997).

[6]United States. Court of Appeals, Ninth Circuit. *Compassion In Dying v. Washington State.* 79 Federal Reporter 3d (1996).

[7]United States. Department of Health and Human Services. National Center for Health Statistics.

[8]Foley, Kathleen, M.D. *Competent Care For The Dying.* The New England Journal Of Medicine, Volume 336, No. 1 (January 2, 1997).

[9]United States. Court of Appeals, Ninth Circuit. *Compassion In Dying v. Washington State.* 79 Federal Reporter 3d (1996).

[10]Ibid.

[11]Ibid.

[12]Ibid.

[13]Ibid.

[14]United States. Supreme Court. *Cruzan v. Director, Missouri Health Dept.* 497 U.S. Reports (1990).

Table Of Contents

Ultimately there comes a point at which the individual's rights overcome the State interest. - N.J. Justice Richard J. Hughes (1976)

The principle that a competent person has a constitutionally protected liberty interest in refusing unwanted medical treatment may be inferred from our prior decisions. - U.S. Justice William Rehnquist (1990)

A competent, terminally ill adult has a constitutionally guaranteed right under the Fourteenth Amendment to commit physician-assisted suicide. - Judge Barbara Rothstein (1994)

In the two hundred and five years of our existence no constitutional right to aid in killing oneself has ever been asserted and upheld by a court of final jurisdiction. - Judge John T. Noonan, Jr. (1995)

Those who believe strongly that death must come without physician assistance are free to follow that creed, be they doctors or patients. They are not free, however, to force their views, their religious convictions, or their philosophies on all the other members of a democratic society, and to compel those whose values differ with theirs to die painful, protracted, and agonizing deaths.
- Judge Stephen Reinhardt (1996)

Section 4: New York's Right-To-Die Decisions
Quill I
139

It is hardly unreasonable or irrational for [New York] State to recognize a difference between allowing nature to take its course, even in the most severe situations, and intentionally using an artificial death-producing device.   - Judge Thomas Griesa (1994)

Quill II
155

The New York statutes criminalizing assisted suicide violate the Equal Protection Clause because, to the extent that they prohibit a physician from prescribing medications to be self-administered by a mentally competent, terminally-ill person in the final stages of his terminal illness, they are not rationally related to any legitimate state interest.   - Judge Roger Miner (1996)

Section 5: The United States Supreme Court's Landmark Decisions In Washington's and New York's Right-To-Die Cases
Washington State v. Glucksberg
179

The history of the law's treatment of assisted suicide in this country has been and continues to be one of the rejection of nearly all efforts to permit it.   - Chief Justice William Rehnquist (1997)

New York State v. Quill
201

Even as the States move to protect and promote patients' dignity at the end of life, they remain opposed to physician-assisted suicide.
    - Chief Justice William Rehnquist (1997)

Bibliography
211

Index
221

The First State Right-To-Die Decision
The *Karen Ann Quinlan* Case

April 15, 1975. For reasons still undetermined, twenty-one-year-old New Jersey resident Karen Ann Quinlan suffers respiratory failure and loses consciousness. Unable to breathe on her own, she is placed on a respirator. Doctors diagnose anoxia, catastrophic brain damage due to lack of oxygen.

July 31, 1975. Karen's parents, Joseph and Julia Quinlan, are told that their is no hope that their daughter will ever emerge from the irreversible coma, called a persistent vegatative state, in which she now lies. They authorize her removal from the respirator.

August 2, 1975. The doctors and hospital, contending that she is not dead by medical standards, refuse the Quinlan's authorization to remove Karen from the respirator.

September 12, 1975. Joseph and Julia Quinlan make an unprecedented petition to the New Jersey Superior Court to make them Karen's legal guardians for the express purpose of removing her from the respirator and ending what they call the hospital's "futile use of extraordinary medical measures." County and State officials, contending that Karen is not dead by legal standards, intercede on the side of the doctors and hospital.

October 20-27, 1975. During trial, the Quinlans argue that Karen has a constitutionally protected right to die, based on the First Amendment (free exercise of religion), the Eighth Amendment (protection against cruel and unusual punishment), and the Fourteenth Amendment (right of privacy). The doctors and hospital counter-argue that they have an obligation to administer medical care to Karen according to their best judgment. The County and State argue that they have a compelling interest in the preservation of Karen's life; they argue that no right to die exists.

November 10, 1975. The New Jersey Superior Court rejects the Quinlan's right-to-die arguments and holds that Karen is alive by both legal and medical standards. Superior Court Judge Robert Muir writes: *The authorization sought [by the Quinlans], if granted, would result in Karen's death. The natural processes of her body are not shown to be sufficiently strong to sustain her by themselves. The authorization, therefore, would permit Karen Quinlan to die. This is not protection. It is not something in her best interests, in a temporal sense, and it is in a temporal sense that I must operate, whether I believe in life after death or not. The single most important temporal quality Karen Ann Quinlan has is life. This court will not authorize that life to be taken from her.*

March 31, 1976. The New Jersey Supreme Court, in a landmark right-to-die decision, overturns the lower court. New Jersey Chief Justice Richard Hughes writes: *Ultimately there comes a point at which the individual's rights overcome the State interest.*

May 17, 1976. Karen is removed from the respirator. Confounding all expert medical opinion, she is able to breathe on her own.

June 11, 1984. Karen Ann Quinlan, comatose for nine years and two months, dies at age thirty.

The original legal text of the New Jersey Supreme Court's landmark right-to-die decision, *In the Matter of Karen Ann Quinlan,* can be found in volume 70 of *New Jersey Reports,* beginning on page 10. Our plain-English edited text follows.

In The Matter Of Karen Ann Quinlan
March 31, 1976

New Jersey Chief Justice Richard J. Hughes: The central figure in this tragic case is Karen Ann Quinlan, a New Jersey resident. At the age of 22, she lies in a debilitated and allegedly moribund state at Saint Clare's Hospital in Denville, New Jersey. The litigation has to do, in final analysis, with her life - its continuance or cessation - and the responsibilities, rights and duties, with regard to any fateful decision concerning it, of her family, her guardian, her doctors, the hospital, the State through its law enforcement authorities, and finally the courts of justice.

. . . . [R]elying on claimed constitutional rights of free exercise of religion, of privacy and of protection against cruel and unusual punishment, Karen Quinlan's father sought judicial authority to withdraw the life-sustaining mechanisms temporarily preserving his daughter's life, and his appointment as guardian of her person to that end. His request was opposed by her doctors, the hospital, the Morris County Prosecutor, the State of New Jersey, and her guardian *ad litem* [an individual appointed by the court as the guardian of her person].

. . . . On the night of April 15, 1975, for reasons still unclear, Karen Quinlan ceased breathing for at least two 15 minute periods. She received some ineffectual mouth-to-mouth resuscitation from friends. She was taken by ambulance to Newton Memorial Hospital. There she had a temperature of 100 degrees, her pupils were unreactive and she was unresponsive even to deep pain. The history at the time of her admission to that hospital was essentially incomplete and uninformative.

Three days later, Dr. [Robert J.] Morse [a neurologist] examined Karen at the request of the Newton admitting physician, Dr. McGee. He found her comatose with evidence of decortication, a condition relating to derangement of the cortex of the brain causing a physical posture in which the upper extremities are flexed and the lower extremities are extended. She required a respirator to assist her breathing. Dr. Morse was unable to obtain an adequate account of the circumstances and events leading up to Karen's admission to the Newton Hospital. Such initial history or etiology is crucial in neurological diagnosis. Relying as he did upon the Newton Memorial records and his own examination, he concluded that prolonged lack of oxygen in the bloodstream, anoxia, was identified with her condition as he saw it upon first observation. When she was later transferred to Saint Clare's Hospital she was still unconscious, still on a respirator and a tracheotomy had been performed. On her arrival Dr. Morse conducted extensive and detailed examinations. An electroencephalogram (EEG) . . . was . . . characterized . . . as "abnormal but it showed some activity and was consistent with her clinical state." Other significant neurological tests . . . were normal in result. Dr. Morse testified that Karen has been in a state of coma, lack of consciousness, since he began treating her. He explained that there are basically two types of coma, sleep-like unresponsiveness and awake unresponsiveness. Karen was originally in a sleeplike unresponsive condition but soon developed "sleep-wake" cycles, apparently a normal improvement for comatose patients occurring within three to four weeks. In the awake cycle she blinks, cries out and does things of that sort but is still totally unaware of anyone or anything around her.

Dr. Morse and other expert physicians who examined her characterized Karen as being in a "chronic persistent vegetative state." . . .

Dr. Morse . . . believed with certainty that Karen Quinlan is not "brain dead." . . .

Because Karen's neurological condition affects her respiratory ability . . . she requires a respirator to assist her breathing. . . . Attempts to "wean" her from the respirator were unsuccessful and have been abandoned.

The experts believe that Karen cannot now survive without the assistance of the respirator; that exactly how long she would live without it is unknown; that the strong likelihood is that death would follow soon after its removal, and that removal would also risk further brain damage and would curtail the assistance the respirator presently provides in warding off infection.

It seemed to be the consensus not only of the treating physicians but also of the several qualified experts who testified in the case, that removal from the respirator would not conform to medical practices, standards and traditions.

. . . . Karen is described as emaciated, having suffered a weight loss of at least 40 pounds, and undergoing a continuing deteriorative process. Her posture is described as fetal-like and grotesque; there is extreme flexion-rigidity of the arms, legs and related muscles and her joints are severely rigid and deformed.

. . . . Severe brain and associated damage . . . has left Karen in a chronic and persistent vegetative state. No form of treatment which can cure or improve that condition is known or available. As nearly as may be determined . . . she can *never* be restored to cognitive or sapient life. . . .

She is debilitated and moribund and although fairly stable at the time of argument before us . . . no physician risked the opinion that she could live more than a year and indeed she may die much earlier. Excellent medical and nursing care so far has been able to ward off the constant threat of infection, to which she is peculiarly susceptible because of the respirator, the tracheal tube and other incidents of care in her vulnerable condition. Her life accordingly is sustained by the respirator and tubal feeding, and removal from the respirator would cause her death soon, although the time cannot be stated with more precision.

. . . . Developments in medical technology have [confused] the use of the traditional definition of death. Efforts have been made to define irreversible coma as a new criterion for death. . . .

The [modern] standards, carefully delineated, included absence of response to pain or other stimuli, pupilary . . . corneal, pharyngeal and other reflexes, blood pressure, spontaneous respiration, as well as "flat" . . . [EEG's] and the like, with all tests repeated "at least 24 hours later with no change." In such circumstances, where all of such criteria have been met as showing "brain death," the [Harvard Medical School Ad Hoc] Committee [which designed these standards] recommends with regard to the respirator:

> . . . . The patient's condition can be determined only by a physician. When the patient is hopelessly damaged as defined above, the family and all colleagues who have participated in major decisions concerning the patient, and all nurses involved, should be so informed. Death is to be declared and *then* the respirator turned off. The decision to do this and the responsibility for it are to be taken by the physician-in-charge, in consultation with one or more physicians who have been directly

involved in the case. It is unsound and undesirable to force the family to make the decision.

But, as indicated, it was the consensus of medical testimony in the [present] case that Karen, for all her disability, met none of these criteria, nor indeed any comparable criteria . . . representing . . . prevailing and accepted medical standards.

We have adverted to the "brain death" concept and Karen's disassociation with any of its criteria, to emphasize the basis of the medical decision made by Dr. Morse. . . . His refusal [to withdraw the life support mechanisms] was based upon his conception of medical standards, practice and ethics. . . .

We agree with the trial court that that decision was in accord with Dr. Morse's conception of medical standards and practice.

We turn to . . . the application for guardianship. . . . The character and general suitability of Joseph Quinlan as guardian for his daughter, in ordinary circumstances, could not be doubted. The record bespeaks the high degree of familial love which pervaded the home of Joseph Quinlan and reached out fully to embrace Karen, although she was living elsewhere at the time of her collapse. The proofs [facts revealed in the trial court] showed him to be deeply religious, imbued with a morality so sensitive that months of tortured indecision preceded his belated conclusion (despite earlier moral judgments reached by the other family members, but unexpressed to him in order not to influence him) to seek the termination of life-supportive measures sustaining Karen. A communicant of the Roman Catholic Church, as were other family members, he first sought solace in private prayer looking with confidence, as he says, to the Creator, first for the recovery of Karen and then, if that were not possible, for guidance with respect to the awesome decision confronting him.

To confirm the moral rightness of the decision he was about to make he consulted with his parish priest and later with the Catholic chaplain of Saint Clare's Hospital. He would not, he testified, have sought termination if that act were to be morally wrong or in conflict with the tenets of the religion he so profoundly respects. He was disabused of doubt, however, when the position of the Roman Catholic Church was made known to him. . . . While it is not usual for matters of religious dogma or concepts to enter a civil litigation . . . they were rightly admitted in evidence here. The judge was bound to measure the character and motivations in all respects of Joseph Quinlan as prospective guardian; and insofar as these religious matters bore upon them, they were properly scrutinized and considered by the court.

. . . . Bishop [Lawrence B.] Casey . . . validated the decision of Joseph Quinlan:

> Competent medical testimony has established that Karen Ann Quinlan has no reasonable hope of recovery from her comatose state by the use of any available medical procedures. The continuance of mechanical (cardiorespiratory) supportive measures to sustain continuation of her body functions and her life constitute extraordinary means of treatment. *Therefore, the decision of Joseph Quinlan to request the discontinuance of this treatment is, according to the teachings of the Catholic Church, a morally correct decision.*

. . . . Before turning to the legal and constitutional issues involved, we feel it essential to reiterate that the "Catholic view" . . . is considered by the Court only in the aspect of its impact upon the conscience, motivation and purpose of the intending guardian, Joseph Quinlan, and not as a precedent [rule established by prior cases] in terms of the civil law.

. . . . [T]he Court confronts and responds to three basic issues:

1. Was the trial court correct in denying the specific relief requested by [Joseph Quinlan], *i.e.*, authorization for termination of the life-supporting apparatus, on the case presented to him? Our determination on that question is in the affirmative.

2. Was the court correct in withholding letters of guardianship from [Joseph Quinlan] and appointing in his stead a stranger? On that issue our determination is in the negative.

3. Should this Court, in the light of the foregoing conclusions, grant . . . relief to [Joseph Quinlan]? On that question our Court's determination is in the affirmative.

. . . . The father of Karen Quinlan is certainly no stranger to the present controversy. His interests are real and adverse and he raises questions of surpassing importance. Manifestly, he has standing [the right] to assert his daughter's constitutional rights, she being incompetent to do so.

. . . . [T]he right to religious beliefs is absolute but conduct in pursuance thereof is not wholly immune from governmental restraint. So it is that, for the sake of life, courts sometimes (but not always) order blood transfusions for Jehovah's Witnesses (whose religious beliefs abhor such procedure), forbid exposure to death from handling virulent snakes or ingesting poison (interfering with deeply held religious sentiments in such regard), and protect the public health as in the case of compulsory vaccination (over the strongest of religious objections). The public interest is thus considered paramount, without essential dissolution of respect for religious beliefs. . . .

Similarly inapplicable to the case before us is the Constitution's Eighth Amendment protection against cruel and unusual punishment which, as held by the trial court, is not relevant to situations other than the imposition of penal sanctions. . . .

It is the issue of the constitutional right of privacy that has given us most concern, in the exceptional circumstances of this case. Here a loving parent . . . raising the rights of his incompetent and profoundly damaged daughter, probably irreversibly doomed to no more than a biologically vegetative remnant of life, is before the court. He seeks authorization to abandon specialized technological procedures which can only maintain for a time a body having no potential for resumption or continuance of other than a "vegetative" existence.

We have no doubt, in these unhappy circumstances, that if Karen were herself miraculously lucid for an interval (not altering the existing prognosis of the condition to which she would soon return) and perceptive of her irreversible condition, she could effectively decide upon discontinuance of the life-support apparatus, even if it meant the prospect of natural death. . . .

We have no hesitancy in deciding . . . that no external compelling interest of the State could compel Karen to endure the unendurable, only to vegetate a few measurable months with no realistic possibility of returning to any semblance of cognitive or sapient life. . . .

Although the Constitution does not explicitly mention a right of privacy, Supreme Court decisions have recognized that a right of personal privacy exists and that certain areas of privacy are guaranteed under the Constitution. . . .

The Court in *Griswold [v. Connecticut]* found the unwritten constitutional right of privacy to exist in the . . . Bill of Rights. . . . Presumably this right is broad enough to encompass a patient's decision to decline medical treatment under certain circumstances, in much the same way as it is broad enough to encompass a woman's decision to terminate pregnancy under certain conditions.

. . . . The claimed interests of the State in this case are essentially the preservation and sanctity of human life and defense of the right of the physician to administer medical treatment according to his best judgment. In this case the doctors say that removing Karen from the respirator will conflict with their professional judgment. [Joseph Quinlan] answers that Karen's present treatment serves only a maintenance function; that the respirator cannot cure or improve her condition but at best can only prolong her inevitable slow deterioration and death; and that the interests of the patient, as seen by her surrogate, the guardian, must be evaluated by the court as predominant, even in the face of an opinion *contra* [against] by the present attending physicians. [Joseph Quinlan]'s distinction is significant. . . . We think that the State's interest [*against*] weakens and the individual's right to privacy grows as the degree of bodily invasion increases and the prognosis dims. Ultimately there comes a point at which the individual's rights overcome the State interest. It is for that reason that we believe Karen's choice, if she were competent to make it, would be vindicated by the law. Her prognosis is extremely poor - she will never resume cognitive life. And the bodily invasion is very great - she requires 24 hour intensive nursing care, antibiotics, the assistance of a respirator, a catheter and feeding tube.

Our affirmation of Karen's independent right of choice, however, would ordinarily be based upon her competency to assert it. The sad truth, however, is that she is grossly incompetent and we cannot discern her supposed choice based on the testimony of her previous conversation with friends. . . . Nevertheless we have concluded that Karen's right of privacy may be asserted on her behalf by her guardian under the peculiar circumstances here present.

. . . . The only practical way to prevent destruction of the right [of privacy] is to permit the guardian and family of Karen to render their best judgment, subject to the qualifications hereinafter stated, as to whether she would exercise it in these circumstances. If their conclusion is in the affirmative this decision should be accepted by a society the overwhelming majority of whose members would, we think, in similar circumstances, exercise such a choice in the same way for themselves or for those closest to them. It is for this reason that we determine that Karen's right of privacy may be asserted in her behalf, in this respect, by her guardian and family under the particular circumstances presented by this record.

. . . . Karen Quinlan is a 22-year-old adult. Her right of privacy in respect of the matter before the Court is to be vindicated by Mr. Quinlan as guardian. . . .

The medical obligation is related to standards and practice prevailing in the profession. The physicians in charge of the case . . . declined to withdraw the respirator. That decision

was consistent with the proofs below [facts established in
the lower court] as to the then existing medical standards
and practices. Under the law as it then stood, Judge Muir
was correct in declining to authorize withdrawal of the respirator.

. . . . We glean from the record here that physicians distinguish between curing the ill and comforting and easing the
dying; that they refuse to treat the curable as if they were
dying or ought to die, and that they have sometimes refused
to treat the hopeless and dying as if they were curable. In
this sense . . . many of them have refused to inflict an unde-
sired prolongation of the process of dying on a patient in
irreversible condition when it is clear that such "therapy"
offers neither human nor humane benefit. . . . [I]n light of
the situation in the present case . . . one would have to
think that the use of [a] respirator or [similar] support could
be considered "ordinary" in the context of the possibly
curable patient but "extraordinary" in the context of the
forced sustaining by cardio-respiratory processes of an irreversibly doomed patient. . . .

Decision-making within health care if it is considered as an
expression of a primary obligation of the physician . . .
should be controlled primarily within the patient-doctor-
family relationship, as indeed was recognized by Judge
Muir. . . .

The evidence in this case convinces us that the focal point
of decision should be the prognosis as to the reasonable
possibility of return to cognitive and sapient life, as distinguished from the forced continuance of that biological
vegetative existence to which Karen seems to be doomed.

. . . . Having concluded that there is a right of privacy that
might permit termination of treatment in the circumstances

of this case, we turn to consider the relationship of the exercise of that right to the criminal law. We are aware that such termination of treatment would accelerate Karen's death. The County Prosecutor and the Attorney General maintain that there would be criminal liability for such acceleration. Under the statutes of this State, the unlawful killing of another human being is criminal homicide. We conclude that there would be no criminal homicide in the circumstances of this case. We believe, first, that the ensuing death would not be homicide but rather expiration from existing natural causes. Secondly, even if it were to be regarded as homicide, it would not be unlawful.

. . . . There is a real . . . distinction between the unlawful taking of the life of another and the ending of artificial life-support systems as a matter of self-determination.

Furthermore, the exercise of a constitutional right such as we have here found is protected from criminal prosecution. We do not question the State's undoubted power to punish the taking of human life, but that power does not encompass individuals terminating medical treatment pursuant to their right of privacy. . . .

The trial judge . . . refus[ed] to appoint Joseph Quinlan to be guardian of the person and limiting his guardianship to that of the property of his daughter. . . .

The trial court was apparently convinced of the high character of Joseph Quinlan and his general suitability as guardian under other circumstances, describing him as "very sincere, moral, ethical and religious." The court felt, however, that the obligation to concur in the medical care and treatment of his daughter would be a source of anguish to him and would distort his "decision-making processes." We disagree, for we sense from the whole record before us that while Mr. Quinlan feels a natural grief, and understandably sorrows because of the tragedy which has befallen his daughter, his strength of purpose and character far out-weighs these sentiments and qualifies him eminently for guardianship of the person as well as the property of his daughter. . . .

We thus arrive at the formulation of the . . . relief which we have concluded is appropriate to this case. Some time has passed since Karen's physical and mental condition was de-scribed to the Court. . . . [W]e assume that she is now even more fragile and nearer to death than she was then. Since her present treating physicians may give reconsideration to her present posture in the light of this opinion, and since we are transferring to [Joseph Quinlan] as guardian the choice of the attending physician and therefore other phy-sicians may be in charge of the case who may take a differ-ent view from that of the present attending physicians, we herewith declare the following . . . relief on behalf of [Joseph Quinlan]. Upon the concurrence of the guardian and family of Karen, should the responsible attending phy-sicians conclude that there is no reasonable possibility of Karen's ever emerging from her present comatose condi-tion to a cognitive, sapient state and that the life-support apparatus now being administered to Karen should be dis-continued, they shall consult with the hospital "Ethics Committee" or like body of the institution in which Karen is then hospitalized. If that consultative body agrees that there is no reasonable possibility of Karen's ever emerging from her present comatose condition to a cognitive, sapient state, the present life-support system may be withdrawn and said action shall be without any civil or criminal liability therefor on the part of any participant, whether guardian, physician, hospital or others. We herewith specifically so hold.

We therefore remand [send back] this record to the trial court to implement . . . the following decisions:

1. To discharge, with the thanks of the Court for his service, the present guardian of the person of Karen Quinlan, Thomas R. Curtin, Esq., a member of the Bar and an officer of the court.

2. To appoint Joseph Quinlan as guardian of the person of Karen Quinlan with full power to make decisions with regard to the identity of her treating physicians. . . .

The First Federal Right-To-Die Decision
The *Nancy Beth Cruzan* Case

January 11, 1983. Responding to the scene of a car accident at 1 a.m., the Missouri Highway Patrol finds 25-five-year-old Nancy Beth Cruzan unconscious, with no heart beat or respiration. At 1:12, paramedics restore her heart and respiration. Permanent brain damage due to lack of oxygen begins after six minutes. Nancy has been without oxygen a minimum of 12 minutes. She falls into an irreversible coma.

February 7, 1983. A feeding tube, used for artificial hydration and nutrition, is surgically implanted into Nancy.

May 1987. Nancy's parents, Lester and Joyce Cruzan, realizing there is no hope that their daughter will ever emerge from the persistent vegetative state in which she lies, request that the State Hospital in which she is a patient disconnect the feeding tube so that she may die. The Missouri Health Department refuses. The Cruzans, as Nancy's co-guardians, bring suit in Jasper County Circuit Court against Robert Harmon, Director of the Health Department.

July 27, 1988. The Jasper County Circuit Court hears the testimony of a friend that Nancy had previously expressed feelings that if she were sick or injured she would not want to continue her life unless she could live "half-way normally." Stating that Nancy's reported comments "suggested" she "would not wish to continue with [artificial] nutrition and hydration," Judge Charles Teel rules that Nancy's "right to liberty" outweighs the State's interest in the preservation of her life, and orders the State Hospital to end their "death prolonging procedures."

November 16, 1988. The Missouri Supreme Court overturns the decision of the Jasper County Circuit Court. It fails to find the testimony concerning Nancy's "suggested" feeling that she did not wish to live if she could not lead a "half-way" normal life as "inherently unreliable." It further finds that the State's interest in the preservation of life outweighs Nancy's "right to liberty." Judge Edward Robertson writes: *The argument made here, that Nancy will not recover, is but a thinly veiled statement that her life in its present form is not worth living. Yet a diminished quality of life does not support a decision to cause death. . . . Nancy is not dead. Her life expectancy is thirty years. . . . If food and water are supplied, she will not die.*

June 25, 1990. The United States Supreme Court, voting 5-4, affirms the decision of the Missouri Supreme Court. They hold that there must be "clear and convincing evidence" of an incompetent person's feeling about the withdrawal of life-sustaining treatment before her guardians are allowed to invoke her constitutionally protected liberty interest to terminate medical treatment. Chief Justice William Rehnquist writes: *The principle that a competent person has a constitutionally protected liberty interest in refusing unwanted medical treatment may be inferred from our prior decisions.*

December 14, 1990. The Jasper County Circuit Court, after hearing new "clear and convincing evidence" of Nancy's feeling about the withdrawal of life-sustaining treatment, orders the disconnection of the feeding tube. The Missouri Health Department withdraws their opposition.

December 26, 1990. Nancy Beth Cruzan, having been comatose for seven years, less sixteen days, dies at age thirty-three, twelve days after the removal of the feeding tube.

The original legal text of the United States Supreme Court's landmark right-to-die decision, *Cruzan v. Director, Missouri Department of Health,* can be found in volume 497 of *United States Reports,* beginning on page 261. Our plain-English edited text follows.

Cruzan v. Missouri
June 25, 1990

Chief Justice William Rehnquist: Petitioner Nancy Beth Cruzan was rendered incompetent as a result of severe injuries sustained during an automobile accident. Copetitioners Lester and Joyce Cruzan, Nancy's parents and co-guardians, sought a court order directing the withdrawal of their daughter's artificial feeding and hydration equipment after it became apparent that she had virtually no chance of recovering her cognitive faculties. The Supreme Court of Missouri held that because there was no clear and convincing evidence of Nancy's desire to have life-sustaining treatment withdrawn under such circumstances, her parents lacked authority to effectuate such a request. We granted certiorari [agreed to review the case], and now affirm [uphold].

On the night of January 11, 1983, Nancy Cruzan lost control of her car as she traveled down Elm Road in Jasper County, Missouri. The vehicle overturned, and Cruzan was discovered lying face down in a ditch without detectable respiratory or cardiac function. Paramedics were able to restore her breathing and heartbeat at the accident site, and she was transported to a hospital in an unconscious state. An attending neurosurgeon diagnosed her as having sustained probable cerebral contusions compounded by significant anoxia (lack of oxygen). The Missouri trial court in this case found that permanent brain damage generally results after 6 minutes in an anoxic state; it was estimated that Cruzan was deprived of oxygen from 12 to 14 minutes. She remained in a coma for approximately three weeks and then progressed to an unconscious state in which she was able to orally ingest some nutrition. In order to ease feeding and further the recovery, surgeons implanted a gastrostomy feeding and hydration tube in Cruzan with the consent of her then husband. Subsequent rehabilitative efforts proved unavailing. She now lies in a Missouri state hospital in what is commonly referred to as a persistent vegetative state: generally, a condition in which a person exhibits motor reflexes but evinces no indications of significant cognitive function. The State of Missouri is bearing the cost of her care.

After it had become apparent that Nancy Cruzan had virtually no chance of regaining her mental faculties her parents asked hospital employees to terminate the artificial nutrition and hydration procedures. All agree that such a removal would cause her death. The employees refused to honor the request without court approval. The parents then sought and received authorization from the state trial court for termination. The court found that a person in Nancy's condition had a fundamental right under the State and Federal Constitutions to refuse or direct the withdrawal of "death prolonging procedures." The court also found that Nancy's "expressed thoughts at age twenty-five in somewhat serious conversation with a housemate friend that if sick or injured she would not wish to continue her life unless she could live at least halfway normally suggests that given her present condition she would not wish to continue on with her nutrition and hydration."

The Supreme Court of Missouri reversed by a divided vote. The court recognized a right to refuse treatment embodied in the common-law doctrine of informed consent, but expressed skepticism about the application of that doctrine in the circumstances of this case. The court also declined to read a broad right of privacy into the State Constitution which would "support the right of a person to refuse medical treatment in every circumstance," and expressed doubt as to whether such a right existed under the United States Constitution. It then decided that the Missouri Living Will statute embodied a state policy strongly favoring the preservation of life. The court found that Cruzan's statements to her roommate regarding her desire to live or die under certain conditions were "unreliable for the purpose of determining her intent, and thus insufficient to support the co-guardians claim to exercise substituted judgment on Nancy's behalf." It rejected the argument that Cruzan's parents were entitled to order the termination of her medical treatment, concluding that "no person can assume that choice for an incompetent in the absence of the formalities required under Missouri's Living Will statutes or the clear and convincing, inherently reliable evidence absent here." The court also expressed its view that "[b]road policy questions bearing on life and death are more properly addressed by representative assemblies" than judicial bodies.

We [agreed] to consider the question of whether Cruzan has a right under the United States Constitution which would require the hospital to withdraw life-sustaining treatment from her under these circumstances.

At common law [law established by custom and usage], even the touching of one person by another without consent and without legal justification was a battery. Before the turn of the century, this Court observed that "[n]o right is held more sacred, or is more carefully guarded, by the common law, than the right of every individual to the possession and control of his own person, free from all restraint or interference of others, unless by clear and unquestionable authority of law." This notion of bodily integrity has been embodied in the requirement that informed consent is generally required for medical treatment. Justice Cardozo, while on the Court of Appeals of New York, aptly described this doctrine: "Every human being of adult years and sound mind has a right to determine what shall be done with his own body; and a surgeon who performs an operation without his patient's consent commits an assault, for which he is liable in damages." The informed consent doctrine has become firmly entrenched in American . . . law.

The logical corollary of the doctrine of informed consent is that the patient generally possesses the right not to consent, that is, to refuse treatment. Until about 15 years ago . . . the number of right-to-refuse-treatment decisions were relatively few. Most of the earlier cases involved patients who refused medical treatment forbidden by their religious beliefs, thus implicating First Amendment rights as well as common law rights of self-determination. More recently, however, with the advance of medical technology capable of sustaining life well past the point where natural forces would have brought certain death in earlier times, cases involving the right to refuse life-sustaining treatment have burgeoned.

In the *Quinlan* case, young Karen Quinlan suffered severe brain damage as the result of anoxia, and entered a persistent vegetative state. Karen's father sought judicial approval to disconnect his daughter's respirator. The New Jersey Supreme Court granted the relief, holding that Karen had a right of privacy grounded in the Federal Constitution to terminate treatment. Recognizing that this right was not absolute, however, the court balanced it against asserted state interests. Noting that the State's interest "weakens and the individual's right to privacy grows as the degree of bodily invasion increases and the prognosis dims," the court concluded that the state interests had to give way in that case. The court also concluded that the "only practical way" to prevent the loss of Karen's privacy right due to her incompetence was to allow her guardian and family to decide "whether she would exercise it in these circumstances."

After *Quinlan,* however, most courts have based a right to refuse treatment either solely on the common law right to informed consent or on both the common law right and a constitutional privacy right. . . .

Many of the later cases build on the principles established in *Quinlan, Saikewicz* and *Storar/Eichner.* For instance, in *In re Conroy,* the same court that decided *Quinlan* considered whether a nasogastric feeding tube could be removed from an 84-year-old incompetent nursing-home resident suffering irreversible mental and physical ailments. While recognizing that a federal right of privacy might apply in the case, the court, contrary to its approach in *Quinlan,* decided to base its decision on the common-law right to self-determination and informed consent. "On balance, the right to self-determination ordinarily outweighs any countervailing state interests, and competent persons generally are permitted to refuse medical treatment, even at the risk of death. Most of the cases that have held otherwise, unless they involved the interest in protecting innocent third parties, have concerned the patient's competency to make a rational and considered choice."

Reasoning that the right of self-determination should not be lost merely because an individual is unable to sense a violation of it, the court held that incompetent individuals retain a right to refuse treatment. It also held that such a right could be exercised by a surrogate decisionmaker using a "subjective" standard when there was clear evidence that the incompetent person would have exercised it. Where such evidence was lacking, the court held that an individual's right could still be invoked in certain circumstances under objective "best interest" standards. Thus, if some trustworthy evidence existed that the individual would have wanted to terminate treatment, but not enough to clearly establish a person's wishes for purposes of the subjective standard, and the burden of a prolonged life from the experience of pain and suffering markedly outweighed its satisfactions, treatment could be terminated under a "limited-objective" standard. Where no trustworthy evidence existed, and a person's suffering would make the administration of life-sustaining treatment inhumane, a "pure-objective" standard could be used to terminate treatment. If none of these conditions obtained, the court held it was best to err in favor of preserving life.

The court also rejected certain categorical distinctions that had been drawn in prior refusal-of-treatment cases as lacking substance for decision purposes: the distinction between actively hastening death by terminating treatment and passively allowing a person to die of a disease; between treating individuals as an initial matter versus withdrawing treatment afterwards; between ordinary versus extraordinary treatment; and between treatment by artificial feeding versus other forms of life-sustaining medical procedures. As to the last item, the court acknowledged the "emotional significance" of food, but noted that feeding by implanted tubes is a "medical procedur[e] with inherent risks and possible side effects, instituted by skilled health-care providers to compensate for impaired physical functioning" which analytically was equivalent to artificial breathing using a respirator.

In contrast to *Conroy*, the Court of Appeals of New York recently refused to accept less than the clearly expressed wishes of a patient before permitting the exercise of her right to refuse treatment by a surrogate decisionmaker. There, the court, over the objection of the patient's family members, granted an order to insert a feeding tube into a 77-year-old woman rendered incompetent as a result of several strokes. While continuing to recognize a common-law right to refuse treatment, the court rejected the substituted judgment approach for asserting it "because it is inconsistent with our fundamental commitment to the notion that no person or court should substitute its judgment as to what would be an acceptable quality of life for another. Consequently, we adhere to the view that, despite its pitfalls and inevitable uncertainties, the inquiry must always be narrowed to the patient's expressed intent, with every effort made to minimize the opportunity for error." The court held that the record lacked the requisite clear and convincing evidence of the patient's expressed intent to withhold life-sustaining treatment.

Other courts have found state statutory law relevant to the resolution of these issues. In *Conservatorship of Drabick,* the California Court of Appeal authorized the removal of a nasogastric feeding tube from a 44-year-old man who was in a persistent vegetative state as a result of an auto accident. . . . [T]he court held that a state probate statute authorized the patient's conservator to order the withdrawal of life-sustaining treatment when such a decision was made in good faith based on medical advice and the conservatee's best interests. . . .

In *In re Estate of Longeway,* the Supreme Court of Illinois considered whether a 76-year-old woman rendered incompetent from a series of strokes had a right to the discontinuance of artificial nutrition and hydration. Noting that the boundaries of a federal right of privacy were uncertain, the court found a right to refuse treatment in the doctrine of informed consent. The court further held that the State Probate Act impliedly authorized a guardian to exercise a ward's right to refuse artificial sustenance in the event that the ward was terminally ill and irreversibly comatose. . . .

As these cases demonstrate, the common-law doctrine of informed consent is viewed as generally encompassing the right of a competent individual to refuse medical treatment. Beyond that, these decisions demonstrate both similarity and diversity in their approach to decision of what all agree is a perplexing question with unusually strong moral and ethical overtones. State courts have available to them for decision a number of sources - state constitutions, statutes, and common law - which are not available to us. In this Court, the question is simply and starkly whether the United States Constitution prohibits Missouri from choosing the rule of decision which it did. This is the first case in which we have been squarely presented with the issue of whether the United States Constitution grants what is in common parlance referred to as a "right to die." We follow the judicious counsel of our decision in *Twin City Bank v. Nebeker*, where we said that in deciding "a question of such magnitude and importance . . . it is the [better] part of wisdom not to attempt, by any general statement, to cover every possible phase of the subject."

The Fourteenth Amendment provides that no State shall "deprive any person of life, liberty, or property, without due process of law." The principle that a competent person has a constitutionally protected liberty interest in refusing unwanted medical treatment may be inferred from our prior decisions. In *Jacobson v. Massachusetts*, for instance, the Court balanced an individual's liberty interest in declining an unwanted smallpox vaccine against the State's interest in preventing disease. Decisions prior to the incorporation of the Fourth Amendment into the Fourteenth Amendment analyzed searches and seizures involving the body under the Due Process Clause and were thought to implicate substantial liberty interests.

Just this Term, in the course of holding that a State's procedures for administering antipsychotic medication to prisoners were sufficient to satisfy due process concerns, we recognized that prisoners possess "a significant liberty interest in avoiding the unwanted administration of antipsychotic drugs under the Due Process Clause of the Fourteenth Amendment." . . .

But determining that a person has a "liberty interest" under the Due Process Clause does not end the inquiry; "whether respondent's constitutional rights have been violated must be determined by balancing his liberty interests against the relevant state interests."

[Cruzan's guardians] insist that . . . the forced administration of life-sustaining medical treatment, and even of artificially-delivered food and water essential to life, would implicate a competent person's liberty interest. Although we think the logic of the cases discussed above would embrace such a liberty interest, the dramatic consequences involved in refusal of such treatment would [answer the question of] whether the deprivation of that interest is constitutionally permissible. But for purposes of this case, we assume that the United States Constitution would grant a competent person a constitutionally protected right to refuse lifesaving hydration and nutrition.

[Cruzan's guardians] go on to assert that an incompetent person should possess the same right in this respect as is possessed by a competent person. They rely primarily on our decisions in *Parham v. J.R.*, and *Youngberg v. Romeo*. In *Parham*, we held that a mentally disturbed minor child had a liberty interest in "not being confined unnecessarily for medical treatment," but we certainly did not intimate that such a minor child, after commitment, would have a liberty interest in refusing treatment. In *Youngberg*, we held that a seriously retarded adult had a liberty interest in safety and freedom from bodily restraint. *Youngberg*, however, did not deal with decisions to administer or withhold medical treatment.

The difficulty with [Cruzan's guardians'] claim is that in a sense it begs the question: an incompetent person is not able to make an informed and voluntary choice to exercise a hypothetical right to refuse treatment or any other right. Such a "right" must be exercised for her, if at all, by some sort of surrogate. Here, Missouri has in effect recognized that under certain circumstances a surrogate may act for the patient in electing to have hydration and nutrition withdrawn in such a way as to cause death, but it has established a procedural safeguard to assure that the action of the surrogate conforms as best it may to the wishes expressed by the patient while competent. Missouri requires that evidence of the incompetent's wishes as to the withdrawal of treatment be proved by clear and convincing evidence. The question, then, is whether the United States Constitution forbids the establishment of this procedural requirement by the State. We hold that it does not.

Whether or not Missouri's clear and convincing evidence requirement comports with the United States Constitution depends in part on what interests the State may properly seek to protect in this situation. Missouri relies on its interest in the protection and preservation of human life, and there can be no gainsaying this interest. As a general matter, the States - indeed, all civilized nations - demonstrate their commitment to life by treating homicide as serious crime. Moreover, the majority of States in this country have laws imposing criminal penalties on one who assists another to commit suicide. We do not think a State is required to remain neutral in the face of an informed and voluntary decision by a physically-able adult to starve to death.

But in the context presented here, a State has more particular interests at stake. The choice between life and death is a deeply personal decision of obvious and overwhelming finality. We believe Missouri may legitimately seek to safeguard the personal element of this choice through the imposition of heightened evidentiary requirements. It cannot be disputed that the Due Process Clause protects an interest in life as well as an interest in refusing life-sustaining medical treatment. Not all incompetent patients will have loved ones available to serve as surrogate decisionmakers. And even where family members are present, "[t]here will, of course, be some unfortunate situations in which family members will not act to protect a patient." A State is entitled to guard against potential abuses in such situations. Similarly, a State is entitled to consider that a judicial proceeding to make a determination regarding an incompetent's wishes may very well not be an adversarial one, with the added guarantee of accurate factfinding that the adversary process brings with it. Finally, we think a State may properly decline to make judgments about the "quality" of life that a particular individual may enjoy, and simply assert an unqualified interest in the preservation of human life to be weighed against the constitutionally protected interests of the individual.

In our view, Missouri has permissibly sought to advance these interests through the adoption of a "clear and convincing" standard of proof to govern such proceedings. "The function of a standard of proof, as that concept is embodied in the Due Process Clause and in the realm of factfinding, is to 'instruct the factfinder concerning the degree of confidence our society thinks he should have in the correctness of factual conclusions for a particular type of adjudication.'" "This Court has mandated an intermediate standard of proof - 'clear and convincing evidence' - when the individual interests at stake in a state proceeding are both 'particularly important' and 'more substantial than mere loss of money.'" Thus, such a standard has been required in deportation proceedings, in denaturalization proceedings, in civil commitment proceedings, and in proceedings for the termination of parental rights. Further, this level of proof, "or an even higher one, has traditionally been imposed in cases involving allegations of civil fraud, and in a variety of other kinds of civil cases involving such issues as . . . lost wills, oral contracts to make bequests, and the like."

We think it self-evident that the interests at stake in the [present] proceedings are more substantial, both on an individual and societal level, than those involved in [an ordinary] dispute. But not only does the standard of proof reflect the importance of a particular adjudication, it also serves as "a societal judgment about how the risk of error should be distributed between the litigants." The more stringent the burden of proof a party must bear, the more that party bears the risk of an erroneous decision. We believe that Missouri may permissibly place an increased risk of an erroneous decision on those seeking to terminate an incompetent individual's life-sustaining treatment. An erroneous decision not to terminate results in a maintenance of the status quo; the possibility of subsequent developments such as advancements in medical science, the discovery of new evidence regarding the patient's intent, changes in the law, or simply the unexpected death of the patient despite the administration of life-sustaining treatment, at least create the potential that a wrong decision will eventually be corrected or its impact mitigated [lessened]. An erroneous decision to withdraw life-sustaining treatment, however, is not susceptible of correction. In *Santosky*, one of the factors which led the Court to require proof by clear and convincing evidence in a proceeding to terminate parental rights was that a decision in such a case was final and irrevocable.

The same must surely be said of the decision to discontinue hydration and nutrition of a patient such as Nancy Cruzan, which all agree will result in her death.

It is also worth noting that most, if not all, States simply forbid oral testimony entirely in determining the wishes of parties in transactions which, while important, simply do not have the consequences that a decision to terminate a person's life does. At common law and by statute in most States, the parole evidence rule prevents the variations of the terms of a written contract by oral testimony. The statute of frauds makes unenforceable oral contracts to leave property by will, and statutes regulating the making of wills universally require that those instruments be in writing. There is no doubt that statutes requiring wills to be in writing, and statutes of frauds which require that a contract to make a will be in writing, on occasion frustrate the effectuation of the intent of a particular decedent, just as Missouri's requirement of proof in this case may have frustrated the effectuation of the not-fully-expressed desires of Nancy Cruzan. But the Constitution does not require general rules to work faultlessly; no general rule can.

In sum, we conclude that a State may apply a clear and convincing evidence standard in proceedings where a guardian seeks to discontinue nutrition and hydration of a person diagnosed to be in a persistent vegetative state. We note that many courts which have adopted some sort of substituted judgment procedure in situations like this, whether they limit consideration of evidence to the prior expressed wishes of the incompetent individual, or whether they allow more general proof of what the individual's decision would have been, require a clear and convincing standard of proof for such evidence.

The Supreme Court of Missouri held that in this case the testimony [offered] at trial did not amount to clear and convincing proof of the patient's desire to have hydration and nutrition withdrawn. In so doing, it reversed a decision of the Missouri trial court which had found that the evidence "suggest[ed]" Nancy Cruzan would not have desired to continue such measures, but which had not adopted the standard of "clear and convincing evidence" enunciated by the Supreme Court. The testimony [offered] at trial consisted primarily of Nancy Cruzan's statements made to a housemate about a year before her accident that she would not want to live should she face life as a "vegetable," and other observations to the same effect. The observations did not deal in terms with withdrawal of medical treatment or of hydration and nutrition. We cannot say that the Supreme Court of Missouri committed constitutional error in reaching the conclusion that it did.

[Cruzan's guardians] alternatively contend that Missouri must accept the "substituted judgment" of close family members even in the absence of substantial proof that their views reflect the views of the patient. They rely primarily upon our decisions in *Michael H. v. Gerald D.* and *Parham v. J.R.* But we do not think these cases support their claim. In *Michael H.* we *upheld* the constitutionality of California's favored treatment of traditional family relationships; such a holding may not be turned around into a constitutional requirement that a State must recognize the primacy of those relationships in a situation like this. And in *Parham*, where the patient was a minor, we also *upheld* the constitutionality of a state scheme in which parents made certain decisions for mentally ill minors. Here again [Cruzan's guardians] would seek to turn a decision which allowed a State to rely on family decisionmaking into a constitutional requirement that the State recognize such decisionmaking. But constitutional law does not work that way.

No doubt is engendered by anything in this record but that Nancy Cruzan's mother and father are loving and caring parents. If the State were required by the United States Constitution to repose a right of "substituted judgment" with anyone, the Cruzans would surely qualify. But we do not think the Due Process Clause requires the State to repose judgment on these matters with anyone but the patient herself. Close family members may have a strong feeling - a feeling not at all ignoble or unworthy, but not entirely disinterested, either - that they do not wish to witness the continuation of the life of a loved one which they regard as hopeless, meaningless, and even degrading. But there is no automatic assurance that the view of close family members will necessarily be the same as the patient's would have been had she been confronted with the prospect of her situation while competent. All of the reasons previously discussed for allowing Missouri to require clear and convincing evidence of the patient's wishes lead us to conclude that the State may choose to defer only to those wishes, rather than confide the decision to close family members.

The judgment of the Supreme Court of Missouri is affirmed [upheld].

Washington's Right-To-Die Decisions
Compassion In Dying v. Washington State

A person is guilty of promoting a suicide attempt when he knowingly causes or aids another person to attempt suicide.
- Washington State's Promoting Suicide Law

On January 29, 1994 the constitutionality of Washington State's Promoting Suicide Law, as it applied specifically to physician-assisted suicide by mentally competent, terminally ill adults in the final stages of their illnesses, was challenged in Federal Court by a coalition of three terminally ill patients, five doctors who regularly treated terminally ill patients, and *Compassion In Dying*, a non-profit organization created to counsel and assist terminally ill patients.

The three terminally ill patients, identified only by these pseudonyms, were: "Jane Roe," a sixty-nine-year-old woman dying of cancer; "John Doe," a forty-four-year-old man dying of AIDS; and "James Poe," a sixty-nine-year-old man dying of cardiac and pulmonary failure. All three terminally ill patients (none of whom survived the litigation) were mentally competent adults in the final stages of their illnesses. All three had requested that their physicians assist them in ending their lives.

The five doctors who regularly treated terminally ill patients were: cancer specialist, Dr. Harold Glucksberg; cardiologist, Dr. Thomas Preston; family practitioners, Dr. Abigail Halperin and Dr. John P. Geyman; and internist, Dr. Peter Shalit. All five doctors had received requests from terminally ill, mentally competent patients in the final stages of their illnesses for assistance in ending their lives.

The non-profit organization assisting terminally ill patients and their families was Compassion In Dying which, under strict guidelines, provided information, counseling, and assistance free of charge to terminally ill, mentally competent adults in the final stage of their illnesses who were considering ending their lives.

Washington State's Promoting Suicide Law, which could trace its legal roots back to the Washington Territory's original 1854 statute against assisted suicide, read in part: **Promoting A Suicide Attempt**: "A person is guilty of promoting a suicide attempt when he knowingly causes or aids another person to attempt suicide. Promoting a suicide attempt is a felony punishable by imprisonment."

The *Compassion In Dying* coalition based their argument for striking down Washington State's Promoting Suicide Law, as it applied to physician-assisted suicide, on two separate provisions of the United States Constitution's Fourteenth Amendment, the Due Process Clause and the Equal Protection Clause.

The Fourteenth Amendment's Due Process Clause states: "No State shall deprive any person of life, liberty, or property without due process of law." The coalition argued that, in interpreting the Due Process Clause, the United States Supreme Court had already said in previous decisions that there were certain intimate and personal choices which were so fundamental to personal liberty (marriage, procreation, contraception, abortion, and the right to refuse medical treatment among them) that government interference was either totally prohibited or sharply limited. They believed that physician-assisted suicide was one of these constitutionally protected personal liberties.

The Fourteenth Amendment's Equal Protection Clause states: "No State shall deny to any person within its jurisdiction the equal protection of the laws." The coalition argued that if, under Washington law, a competent adult could, after consulting with a doctor, legally refuse life sustaining medical treatment, then it was a violation of the Equal Protection Clause to make it illegal to commit suicide with the aid and assistance of a doctor.

The State of Washington, represented by their Attorney General, argued that neither the Fourteenth Amendment's Due Process nor Equal Protection Clauses overcame these important State interests in preventing the legalization of physician-assisted suicide: preserving life; preventing suicide; avoiding the involvement of third parties, and precluding the use of arbitrary, unfair, or undue influence; the effect on children, other family members, and loved ones; protecting the integrity of the medical profession; and fear of adverse consequences.

On May 3, 1994, Chief Judge Barbara Rothstein of the United States District Court for the Western District of Washington issued a decision in *Compassion In Dying v. Washington State* (*Compassion I*). Judge Rothstein struck down Washington State's Promoting Suicide Law as an unconstitutional violation of both the Fourteenth Amendment's Due Process Clause, by placing upon terminally ill patients and their physicians an undue burden on the exercise of their constitutionally protected liberty, and Equal Protection Clause, by impermissibly treating similar groups of terminally ill patients differently.

The State of Washington appealed for a reversal of the District Court decision to the United States Court of Appeals, Ninth Circuit.

A three-judge appeals panel heard oral arguments from all parties on December 7, 1994 and on March 9, 1995 issued their 2-1 decision in *Compassion In Dying v. Washington State* (*Compassion II*). Judge John Noonan, writing for the Ninth Circuit Court of Appeals, reversed the District Court decision, finding neither in the Fourteenth Amendment's Equal Protection nor Due Process Clauses the right to physician-assisted suicide.

The *Compassion In Dying* coalition appealed for a rehearing of the 2-1 decision of the three-judge panel by the entire Appeals Court. The United States Court of Appeals, Ninth Circuit, because of what they termed "the extraordinary importance of the case," granted their request on August 1, 1995.

An eleven-judge panel heard oral arguments from all parties on October 26, 1995 and on March 6, 1996 issued their decision in *Compassion In Dying v. Washington State* (*Compassion III*). Circuit Judge Stephen Reinhardt, writing for the Ninth Circuit Court of Appeals, affirmed the District Court decision, based only on the Due Process Clause.

The original legal text of the United States District Court's decision in *Compassion In Dying v. Washington State* (*Compassion I*) can be found in volume 850 of the *Federal Supplement*, beginning on page 1455. Our plain-English edited text begins on page 39.

The original legal text of the United States Court of Appeals' first decision in *Compassion In Dying v. Washington State* (*Compassion II*) can be found in volume 49 of the *Federal Reporter, 3d Series*, beginning on page 586. Our plain-English edited text begins on page 59.

The original legal text of the United States Court of Appeals' second decision in *Compassion In Dying v. Washington State* (*Compassion III*) can be found in volume 79 of the *Federal Reporter, 3d Series*, beginning on page 790. Our plain-English edited text begins on page 73.

Compassion In Dying v. Washington State
May 3, 1994

Chief Judge Barbara Rothstein: This court is asked to rule as a matter of first impression on the constitutionality of the State of Washington's criminal prohibition against physician-assisted suicide. Specifically, the plaintiffs [a coalition of three terminally ill patients, five physicians who regularly treat the terminally ill, and a non-profit counseling organization for the terminally ill] assert that the Fourteenth Amendment to the United States Constitution guarantees adults who are mentally competent, terminally ill, and acting under no undue influence the right to voluntarily hasten their death by taking a lethal dose of physician-prescribed drugs. [The p]laintiffs accordingly challenge the constitutionality of [Washington's criminal prohibition against assisted suicide], which makes it a felony to knowingly aid another person in committing suicide. [The p]laintiffs challenge the statute only insofar as it bans physician-assisted suicide by mentally competent, terminally ill adults who knowingly and voluntarily choose to hasten their death.

The plaintiffs seek both a . . . judgment striking down [the State of Washington's statute prohibiting physician-assisted suicide] as unconstitutional, and injunctive relief barring [the] State of Washington and the Washington Attorney General from enforcing the statute. . . .

The plaintiffs are a coalition of three terminally ill patients, five physicians who treat terminally ill patients, and Compassion in Dying, an organization which provides support, counseling and assistance to mentally competent, terminally ill adults considering suicide.

Jane Roe is a 69-year-old retired pediatrician who has suffered since 1988 from cancer which has now metastasized throughout her skeleton. Although she tried and benefitted temporarily from various treatments including chemotherapy and radiation, she is now in the terminal phase of her disease. In November of 1993, her doctor referred her to hospice care. Only patients with a life expectancy of less than six months are eligible for such care.

Jane Roe has been almost completely bedridden since June of 1993 and experiences constant pain, which becomes especially sharp and severe when she moves. The only medical treatment available to her at this time is medication, which cannot fully alleviate her pain. In addition, she suffers from swollen legs, bed sores, poor appetite, nausea and vomiting, impaired vision, incontinence of bowel, and general weakness.

Jane Roe is mentally competent and wishes to hasten her death by taking prescribed drugs with the help of plaintiff Compassion in Dying. In keeping with the requirements of that organization, she has made three requests for its members to provide her and her family with counseling, emotional support and any necessary ancillary assistance at the time she takes the drugs.

John Doe is a 44-year-old artist dying of AIDS. Since his diagnosis in 1991, he has experienced two bouts of pneumonia, chronic, severe skin and sinus infections, grand mal seizures and extreme fatigue. He has already lost 70% of his vision to cytomegalovirus retinitis, a degenerative disease which will result in blindness and rob him of his ability to paint. His doctor has indicated that he is in the terminal phase of his illness.

John Doe is especially cognizant of the suffering imposed by a lingering terminal illness because he was the primary caregiver for his long-term companion who died of AIDS in June of 1991. He also observed his grandfather's death from diabetes preceded by multiple amputations as well as loss of vision and hearing. Mr. Doe is mentally competent, understands there is no cure for AIDS, and wants his physician to prescribe drugs which he can use to hasten his death.

James Poe is a 69-year-old retired sales representative who suffers from emphysema, which causes him a constant sensation of suffocating. He is connected to an oxygen tank at all times, and takes morphine regularly to calm the panic reaction associated with his feeling of suffocation. Mr. Poe also suffers from heart failure related to his pulmonary disease which obstructs the flow of blood to his extremities and causes severe leg pain. There are no cures for his pulmonary and cardiac conditions, and he is in the terminal phase of his illness. Mr. Poe is mentally competent and wishes to commit suicide by taking physician-prescribed drugs.

The five physician plaintiffs all regularly treat terminally ill patients. Dr. Harold Glucksberg is an assistant professor of medicine at the University of Washington School of Medicine and practices oncology, the treatment of cancer, at the Pacific Medical Center in Seattle. He has published dozens of articles in medical journals dealing with cancer.

In his declaration to the court, Dr. Glucksberg states:

> Cancer usually progresses steadily and slowly. The cancer patient is fully aware of his or her present suffering and anticipates certain future suffering. The terminal cancer patient faces a future that can

be terrifying. Near the end, the cancer patient is usually bedridden, rapidly losing mental and physical functions, often in excruciating, unrelenting pain. Pain management at this stage often requires the patient to choose between enduring unrelenting pain or surrendering an alert mental state because the dose of drugs adequate to alleviate the pain will impair consciousness. Many patients will choose one or the other of these options; however, some patients do not want to end their days either racked with pain or in a drug-induced stupor. For some patients pain cannot be managed even with aggressive use of drugs.

Dr. John P. Geyman was a professor and chair of the Department of Family Medicine at the University of Washington School of Medicine from 1976 through 1990. He is currently a professor emeritus at the University of Washington and has a private practice in family medicine. Dr. Geyman has published over seventy articles regarding family medicine in medical journals, has written several books in the field, was the founding editor of the *Journal of Family Practice*, and has served as editor since 1990 of the *Journal of the American Board of Family Practice*. Dr. Geyman states to the court that,

> in the presence of terminal illness, the shared goal of medical care at some point becomes comfort care rather than cure.

> With advancing medical technology, many patients are subject to active and ineffective therapeutic efforts by their physicians, even when an early terminal outcome is not in doubt. As a result, many experience prolonged deaths often involving pain, suffering and loss of dignity. In reaction to this

problem, an increasing number of patients want more direct control over the type of care they receive in the last stage of their lives. A subset of dying patients desire to shorten their dying process and thereby avoid a lingering death and associated pain, suffering and loss of dignity.

Terminally ill persons who seek to hasten death by consuming drugs need medical counseling. . . . Knowing what drug, in what amount, will hasten death for a particular patient, in light of the patient's medical condition and medication regimen, is a complex medical task.

It is not uncommon, in light of present legal constraints on physician assistance, that patients seeking to hasten their deaths try to do so without medical advice. These efforts are often unsuccessful and can cause the patient and family increased anxiety, pain and suffering. Very often, patients who survive a failed suicide attempt find themselves in worse shape than before the attempt.

Dr. Thomas A. Preston is currently chief of the cardiology unit at Pacific Medical Center in Seattle. He has published numerous articles and books in the field of cardiology, and has received numerous honors for medical teaching and writing. Dr. Preston regularly treats patients dying from cardiopulmonary diseases, a process which can last several months. Dr. Abigail Halperin practices family medicine and occasionally treats patients with terminal illnesses including cancer and AIDS. Dr. Peter Shalit practices general internal medicine; a substantial number of his patients suffer from HIV infection and AIDS. Both Dr. Halperin and Dr. Shalit are also clinical instructors at the University of Washington School of Medicine.

The five physician plaintiffs all state that they have received requests from terminally ill, mentally competent patients in the final stage of their diseases who wished assistance in hastening death. Although their professional judgments have at times dictated that they should assist such patients, they have all been deterred from doing so by the existence of the Washington statute challenged in this case.

Compassion in Dying is a Washington non-profit organization which provides information, counseling and assistance free of charge to mentally competent, terminally ill adult patients considering suicide and to the families of such patients.

Compassion in Dying operates under a written protocol and has strict eligibility requirements for the individuals to whom it provides services. Eligible patients must be considered terminally ill in the judgment of the primary care physician and must be capable of understanding their own decisions. Evaluation by a mental health professional may be obtained to insure that the patient's request is not motivated by depression, emotional distress or mental illness. A request for assisted suicide must not be the result of inadequate comfort care, nor can it be motivated by a lack of adequate health insurance or other economic concerns. The request must come from the patient personally, in writing or on videotape, and must be repeated three times, with an interval of at least 48 hours between the second and third requests. Requests may not be made through advance directives or by a health care surrogate, attorney-in-fact or any other person.

According to its guidelines, Compassion in Dying will not assist anyone to commit suicide who expresses any ambivalence or uncertainty. If the patient has immediate family members or other close personal friends, their approval must be obtained. If any members of the immediate family express disapproval, Compassion in Dying will not provide assistance with suicide. As an additional safeguard, Compassion in Dying requires the patient to provide medical records. A consulting physician must review them to verify the patient's terminal prognosis and decision-making capability as well as to rule out inadequate pain management as the reason for requesting assisted suicide.

Defendants [the State of Washington and the Attorney General of Washington] do not contest the factual declarations by the various plaintiffs, except to deny that the physicians' personal statements of their professional standards are in accord with either the ethical standards or the licensing laws applicable to their profession.

Washington has no law prohibiting suicide or attempted suicide. However, Washington bans aiding or causing the suicide of another:

> A person is guilty of promoting a suicide attempt when he knowingly causes or aids another person to attempt suicide.

> Promoting a suicide attempt is a . . . felony punishable by imprisonment for a maximum of five years and a fine of up to ten thousand dollars.

All of the plaintiffs assert a facial challenge to the constitutionality of [Washington's law] prohibiting assisted suicide. However, plaintiffs' specific claims vary because of their differing circumstances. Jane Roe, John Doe and James Poe allege that they, as mentally competent, terminally ill adults with no chance of recovery, have a constitutionally protected liberty interest under the Fourteenth Amendment which gives them the right to commit physician-assisted suicide without undue governmental interference. Thus, they challenge the constitutionality of the statute insofar as it bars physicians from aiding informed, mentally competent, terminally ill adults to commit suicide. They also attack the statute on equal protection grounds.

The plaintiff physicians assert claims on behalf of their mentally competent, terminally ill adult patients who seek to commit suicide with drugs prescribed for that purpose. The physicians also allege that the Fourteenth Amendment protects their right to practice medicine consistent with their best professional judgment, including the right to assist competent, terminally ill adult patients to hasten death by prescribing suitable medication for self-administration by the patient.

Compassion in Dying's alleged organizational purpose is to assist competent, terminally ill adults who wish to commit suicide by self-administering prescription medication. Compassion in Dying contends that such persons have the right to request assistance from its staff members, including counseling and delivering or mixing the drugs that are to be used. Under current Washington law prohibiting any form of assisted suicide, Compassion in Dying fears that it may be criminally prosecuted for its activities in assisting dying persons as they exercise their alleged constitutional right to hasten their own deaths.

The Fourteenth Amendment to the United States Constitution declares that the state may not "deprive any person of life, liberty, or property, without due process of law." Plaintiffs assert the existence of a liberty interest protected by the Fourteenth Amendment which extends to a personal choice by a mentally competent, terminally ill adult to commit physician-assisted suicide. They contend that individuals in those circumstances have a constitutionally protected right to be free from undue governmental intrusion on their decision to hasten death and avoid prolonged suffering.

The United States Supreme Court has established through a long line of cases that personal decisions relating to marriage, procreation, contraception, family relationships, child rearing and education are constitutionally protected. As explained in [*Planned Parenthood v.*] *Casey*,

> [t]hese matters, involving the most intimate and personal choices a person may make in a lifetime, choices central to personal dignity and autonomy, are central to the liberty protected by the Fourteenth Amendment. At the heart of liberty is the right to define one's own concept of existence, of meaning, of the universe, and of the mystery of human life. Beliefs about these matters could not define the attributes of personhood were they formed under compulsion of the State.

The opinion in *Casey* involved a woman's right to choose abortion, and thus did not address the question of what liberty interest may inhere in a terminally ill person's choice to commit suicide. However, this court finds the reasoning in *Casey* highly instructive and almost prescriptive on the latter issue. Like the abortion decision, the decision of a terminally ill person to end his or her life "involv[es] the most intimate and personal choices a person may make in a lifetime" and constitutes a "choice[ ] central to personal dignity and autonomy."

The court in *Casey* spoke of the suffering of the pregnant woman, which "is too intimate and personal for the State to insist, without more, upon its own vision of the woman's role, however dominant that vision has been in the course of our history and our culture." *Casey* further acknowledged the deep, heart-felt differences of opinion about the morality of abortion, but recognized that the court's duty is not to impose a particular moral standard:

> Some of us as individuals find abortion offensive to our most basic principles of morality, but that cannot control our decision. Our obligation is to define the liberty of all, not to mandate our own moral code. The underlying constitutional issue is whether the State can resolve these philosophic questions in such a definitive way that a woman lacks all choice in the matter. . . .

This court is well aware of the similarly divisive controversy about the appropriateness of suicide by the terminally ill. But the underlying constitutional issue is whether the State of Washington can resolve the profound spiritual and moral questions surrounding the end of life in so conclusive a fashion as to deny categorically any option for a terminally ill, mentally competent person to commit physician-assisted suicide. This court concludes that the suffering of a terminally ill person cannot be deemed any less intimate or personal, or any less deserving of protection from unwarranted governmental interference, than that of a pregnant woman. Thus, consonant with the reasoning in *Casey*, such an intimate personal decision falls within the realm of the liberties constitutionally protected under the Fourteenth Amendment.

Defendants point out that the Washington State legislature might, in the future, decide to amend the statute prohibiting all assisted suicide so as to make an exception for physician-assisted suicide. Defendants strongly urge the court to leave this decision to the State legislature, which will in turn reflect the will of the people living in Washington. But where a constitutional right is involved, this court simply may not abdicate its responsibility to face the issue, no matter how difficult or divisive. Under those circumstances, this court is legally bound to recognize the right and determine how it affects the outcome of the case before it.

Defendants also argue that the *Casey* analysis is inapposite because there are significant differences between reproductive rights and assisted suicide. First, defendants contend that the level of personal autonomy is greater in the area of reproductive rights because of the greater level of control that humans have historically been able to exercise over the beginning of life, as opposed to the end of life, which usually results from forces outside individual control. Assuming that defendants' observation is correct, this hardly amounts to a distinction that warrants a different constitutional result.

Second, defendants contend that the competing interests differ in cases involving reproductive rights and assisted suicide. In the former, the ongoing life interest of the woman is pitted against the potential life interest of the fetus. In the latter, the interests of the person who wishes to take his or her own life must be weighed against the interests of similarly situated persons who might be subject to undue influence if assisted suicide were allowed.

The court agrees that the competing interests differ, but concludes that if any comparison can be made between the two types of decisions, both of which are emotionally complicated and fraught with social implications, the abortion situation raises *more* difficult questions about competing interests. In reproductive rights cases, there is not only the interest of the pregnant woman seeking an abortion, but also the potential life interest which cannot speak for itself. By contrast, in the case of assisted suicide involving a competent person, only one life is involved and that individual can voice his or her wishes.

Third, defendants contend that any system allowing assisted suicide would create the potential for abuse and undue influence, whereas recognizing a right to abortion does not raise the specter of undue influence from others with regard to making a decision to abort. This argument is unpersuasive. One can readily imagine many situations in which a pregnant woman or girl could be subjected to intense pressure from others to get an abortion.

Finally, defendants maintain that reproductive rights analysis differs from assisted suicide issues because of the difference in the level of medical knowledge between the two situations. According to defendants, much more is known about the medical possibilities at the beginning of life than at the end. Even assuming the truth of defendants' argument, it is irrelevant. *Casey* and its progenitors did not base the right to choose abortion on the level of medical knowledge about human reproduction, but on the idea that there is a constitutionally protected "realm of personal liberty which the government may not enter." The question for this court is whether the choice to commit physician-assisted suicide falls within that realm. This determination is not dependent on advancements in medical science.

In addition to *Casey*, the court also finds *Cruzan v. Director, Missouri Dept. of Health* instructive. In *Cruzan*, the Supreme Court considered whether a competent person has a constitutionally protected liberty interest in refusing unwanted, life-sustaining medical treatment including artificially delivered food and water essential to life. In his majority opinion, Justice Rehnquist acknowledged that this principle "may be inferred from our prior decisions," and that "the logic of the cases . . . would embrace such a liberty interest." He then assumed for purposes of the case before the Court "that the United States Constitution would grant a competent person a constitutionally protected right to refuse lifesaving hydration and nutrition."

This court is confident that, squarely faced with the issue, the Supreme Court would reaffirm Justice Rehnquist's tentative conclusion in *Cruzan* that a competent person has a protected liberty interest in refusing unwanted medical treatment, even when that treatment is life-sustaining and refusal or withdrawal of the treatment would mean certain death. The question then becomes whether a constitutional distinction can be drawn between refusal or withdrawal of medical treatment which results in death, and the situation in this case involving competent, terminally ill individuals who wish to hasten death by self-administering drugs prescribed by a physician. In other words, is there a difference for purposes of finding a Fourteenth Amendment liberty interest between refusal of unwanted treatment which will result in death and committing physician-assisted suicide in the final stage of life?

The liberty interest protected by the Fourteenth Amendment is the freedom to make choices according to one's individual conscience about those matters which are essential to personal autonomy and basic human dignity. There is no more profoundly personal decision, nor one which is closer to the heart of personal liberty, than the choice which a terminally ill person makes to end his or her suffering and hasten an inevitable death. From a constitutional perspective, the court does not believe that a distinction can be drawn between refusing life-sustaining medical treatment and physician-assisted suicide by an uncoerced, mentally competent, terminally ill adult.

Based on the reasoning set forth in *Casey* and *Cruzan*, the court concludes that a competent, terminally ill adult has a constitutionally guaranteed right under the Fourteenth Amendment to commit physician-assisted suicide.

. . . . Defendants cite two primary interests furthered by the challenged statute: preventing suicide and protecting those at risk of suicide from undue influence from others who would aid them in completing the act.

In support of the first interest, prevention of suicide, [the State of Washington] point[s] to statistics concerning the rate of suicide in Washington among various age groups, particularly the young. Obviously, the State has a strong, legitimate interest in deterring suicide by young people and others with a significant natural life span ahead of them.

But this case is not about people for whom suicide would abruptly cut life short. Plaintiffs in this case are people suffering through the final stage of life with no hope of recovery. As to them, preventing suicide simply means prolonging a dying person's suffering, an aim in which the State can have no interest. In other words, the State's legitimate interest in preventing suicide is not abrogated by allowing mentally competent, terminally ill patients to freely and voluntarily commit physician-assisted suicide.

The State's interest in preventing suicide by prohibiting any manner of assisted suicide in actuality arises out of its apprehension of the "slippery slope" problem. The State is concerned that allowing any exception to a total ban will encourage the gradual development of a more permissive attitude toward suicide. That attitude, the State fears, will in turn erode the societal constraints now hindering people from committing suicide themselves or countenancing the thought as an appropriate course of action for others, and will result in more suicides by those temporarily depressed, distraught or mentally disturbed.

The court recognizes the tragedy involved when, for example, suicide ends a young life that, with timely and appropriate counseling, could have continued. But despite the general validity of the State's concern, the slippery slope argument cannot prevail in this instance. It may be difficult to define the kinds of assistance which are necessary and should be permitted in order to honor terminally ill patients' protected liberty interest in hastening their death. However, that is not a sufficient excuse for precluding *entirely* the exercise of a constitutional right. The court has no doubt that the legislature can devise regulations which will define the appropriate boundaries of physician-assisted suicide for terminally ill individuals, and at the same time give due recognition to the important public policy concerns regarding the prevention of suicide.

The State's second stated interest, protecting people from committing suicide due to undue influence or duress, is also unquestionably a legitimate consideration. But it is undisputed that plaintiffs in this case are mentally competent individuals who have reached a decision to commit physician-assisted suicide free of any undue influence. Thus, the plaintiffs and others who make knowing and voluntary choices to commit physician-assisted suicide by definition fall outside the realm of the State's concern.

Moreover, Washington State law permits an individual to refuse or require the withdrawal of life-sustaining treatment. Finally, Washington law also recognizes that decisions about life-sustaining medical treatment may be exercised by an authorized representative holding a durable power of attorney for health care.

The potential risk of abuse and undue influence is often just as great and may be greater in certain cases for a patient who requests to be disconnected from a life-support system. The risk of abuse is especially present if the patient is incompetent and a surrogate is making the decision.

As discussed above, the court must determine pursuant to the *Casey* undue burden standard whether the challenged statute "has the purpose or effect of placing a substantial obstacle in the path" of a person seeking to commit physician-assisted suicide. According to the *Casey* standard, a statute with this purpose is invalid because the means chosen by the state to further its interest in preventing undue influence "must be calculated to inform the person's free choice, not hinder it." Moreover, "a statute which, while furthering . . . [a] valid state interest, has the effect of placing a substantial obstacle in the path of a woman's choice cannot be considered a permissible means of serving its legitimate ends."

In this case, the challenged statute not only places a substantial obstacle in the path of a terminally ill, mentally competent person wishing to commit physician-assisted suicide, but entirely prohibits it. There is no question that such a total ban places an undue burden on the exercise of a constitutionally protected liberty interest.

The court finds that neither of the two alleged State interests, preventing suicide and protecting people against undue influence from others, would be impeded by allowing physician-assisted suicide for mentally competent, terminally ill adult patients. By reaching this conclusion, the court does not mean to dismiss the importance or legitimacy of the State's interests in deterring suicide or to suggest that the state has no ability to regulate assisted suicide. Clearly, the State can regulate in this area as long as the regulation does not constitute an undue burden on the exercise of a constitutional right and is reasonably related to a legitimate state interest.

In this case specifically, the court recognizes the legitimacy of the State's interest in preventing undue influence by third parties who may seek to coerce or manipulate a person into committing suicide. But this concern can be answered by devising safeguards and imposing restrictions on physician-assisted suicide to ensure the knowing and voluntary nature of the decision. It is well within the legislative prerogative to enact regulations and restrictions which will ensure that undue influence from third parties plays no part in the choice of physician-assisted suicide.

Plaintiffs also assert that [the Washington law banning physician-assisted suicide] denies them equal protection of the law as guaranteed by the United States Constitution. The Equal Protection Clause of the Fourteenth Amendment "is essentially a direction that all persons similarly situated should be treated alike." When state laws infringe on constitutionally protected personal rights of some people, but not others similarly situated, those laws are subjected to strict scrutiny and will be sustained only if the classifications are suitably tailored to serve a compelling state interest.

Plaintiffs in this case contend that Washington State law unconstitutionally distinguishes between two similarly situated groups of mentally competent, terminally ill adults. Under current state law, those terminally ill persons whose condition involves the use of life-sustaining equipment may lawfully obtain medical assistance in terminating such treatment, including food and water, and thereby hasten death, while those who also suffer from terminal illnesses, but whose treatment does not involve the use of life support systems, are denied the option of hastening death with medical assistance.

Defendants argue that the distinction between the two groups of competent, terminally ill adults does not violate the Fourteenth Amendment's guarantee of equal protection because death resulting from the removal of life support systems is "natural" and death resulting from medical assistance other than removal of life support is "artificial." Defendants assert that the governmental interest in preventing suicide is "not implicated in an individual's refusal of life sustaining treatment," but *is* implicated in the context of physician-assisted suicide, and that the compelling state interest requirement is therefore satisfied.

The court finds the two groups of mentally competent, terminally ill adults at issue here to be similarly situated. While the court recognizes that the governmental interest in preventing suicide is a compelling state interest, Washington caselaw and the Washington Natural Death Act have already carved out an exception for terminally ill patients, and others, wishing to terminate life support. Thus, the State has already recognized that its interest in preventing suicide does not require an absolute ban.

This court is not persuaded that the distinction between "natural" and "artificial" death justifies disparate treatment of these similarly situated groups. The distinction between the terminally ill patient who requests that her physician remove the life support systems necessary to maintain her life, and the terminally ill patient whose condition does not require life support systems but who seeks physician-administered aid to end her life, is not a narrowly-drawn classification tailored to serve a compelling state interest. Both patients may be terminally ill, suffering pain and loss of dignity and subjected to a more extended dying process without some medical intervention, be it removal of life support systems or the prescription of medication to be self-administered.

Washington law, by creating an exception for those patients on life support, yet not permitting competent, terminally ill adult patients such as plaintiffs the equivalent option of exercising their rights to hasten their deaths with medical assistance, creates a situation in which the fundamental rights of one group are burdened while those of a similarly situated group are not. Therefore, this court finds that [the Washington law banning physician-assisted suicide] violates the equal protection guarantee of the Fourteenth Amendment.

. . . . The court declares [the Washington law banning physician-assisted suicide] unconstitutional because it places an undue burden on the exercise of a protected Fourteenth Amendment liberty interest by terminally ill, mentally competent adults acting knowingly and voluntarily, without undue influence from third parties, who wish to commit physician-assisted suicide. The court further declares [the Washington law banning physician-assisted suicide] unconstitutional because it violates the right to equal protection under the Fourteenth Amendment by prohibiting physician-assisted suicide while permitting the refusal or withdrawal of life support systems for terminally ill individuals.

The motion for summary judgment filed by plaintiffs Jane Roe, John Doe and James Poe is accordingly granted, and defendants' cross-motion for summary judgment as to those claims is denied. The physician plaintiffs' motion for summary judgment is granted insofar as the physicians purport to raise claims on behalf of their terminally ill patients. The physician plaintiffs' motion for summary judgment is denied as to their own claims on the grounds that the basis for those claims has not been adequately addressed. For the same reason, plaintiff Compassion in Dying's claim on its own behalf is denied at this time.

As for the injunctive relief requested by plaintiffs, the court declines to enter an injunction barring defendants from enforcing [the Washington ban on physician-assisted suicide].

Compassion in Dying v. Washington State
March 9, 1995

Circuit Judge John T. Noonan, Jr.: The State of Washington appeals the decision of the district court holding unconstitutional Washington's statute on promoting a suicide attempt. Finding no basis for concluding that the statute violates the Constitution, we reverse the district court.

The challenged statute reads as follows:

Promoting a suicide attempt

(1) A person is guilty of promoting a suicide attempt when he knowingly causes or aids another person to attempt suicide.
(2) Promoting a suicide is a Class C felony.

Compassion in Dying is a nonprofit incorporated in the state of Washington. Its avowed purpose is to assist persons described by it as "competent" and "terminally ill" to hasten their deaths by providing them information, counselling, and emotional support but not by administering fatal medication.

Three individuals were plaintiffs in their own right. Their identities are cloaked by an order permitting them to litigate under pseudonyms. They are now deceased. Jane Roe was a 69-year-old physician, suffering from cancer; she had been bedridden for seven months at the time the suit was brought and died before judgment was entered by the district court. John Doe was a 44-year-old artist, who was partially blind at the time of suit and was also suffering from AIDS; he had been advised that his disease was incurable; he died prior to judgment. James Poe was a 69-

year-old patient suffering from chronic obstructive pulmonary disease; he was connected to an oxygen tank at all times. He died after judgment but prior to the hearing of this appeal.

Four physicians also joined the suit asserting their own rights and those of their patients. Harold Glucksberg has specialized in the care of cancer since 1985 and is a clinical assistant professor at the University of Washington School of Medicine. According to his sworn declaration, he "occasionally" encounters patients whom he believes he should assist in terminating their lives, but does not because of the statute; he refers to two such patients, both deceased. Abigail Halpern is the medical director of Uptown Family Practice in Seattle and serves as a clinical faculty member at the University of Washington School of Medicine. In her practice, according to her sworn declaration, she "occasionally" treats patients dying of cancer or AIDS, whose death she believes she should hasten but does not because of the statute; she refers to one such patient, now deceased. Thomas A. Preston is chief of cardiology at Pacific Medical Center in Seattle and professor of Medicine at the University of Washington School of Medicine. According to his sworn declaration, he "occasionally" treats patients whose death he believes he should hasten but does not on account of the statute; he refers to one such patient, now deceased. Peter Shalit is in private practice in Seattle and the medical director of the Seattle Gay Clinic; he is a clinical instructor at the University of Washington School of Medicine. According to his sworn declaration, he "occasionally" treats patients whose death he believes he should hasten, but does not on account of the statute; he refers to one such patient, now deceased.

On January 29, 1994, the plaintiffs brought suit against Washington, seeking a declaration that the statute [prohibiting physician-assisted suicide] violated . . . the Constitution of the United States. . . .

The plaintiffs introduced the declarations of the physicians already noted, together with declarations from the executive director of Compassion in Dying and from Jane Roe, John Doe, and James Poe. They also introduced the sworn declaration of John P. Geyman, who had served from 1976 through 1990 as professor and chairman of the Department of Family Medicine at the School of Medicine of the University of Washington and is now engaged in rural practice at Friday Harbor. According to him, there is "often a severe adverse emotional and psychological effect" on patients unable because of the statute to broach the subject of their desire to hasten their deaths or who do broach the subject and are rebuffed.

. . . . On May 3, 1994, the district court . . . declared the statute to violate the Constitution of the United States.

The district court reached its conclusion as to unconstitutionality on two grounds. First, the court held that the statute violated the liberty guaranteed by the Fourteenth Amendment against deprivation by a state. The court reached this conclusion by noting "a long line of cases" protecting "personal decisions relating to marriage, procreation, contraception, family relationships, child rearing and education." The court quoted as the explanation of this line the statement made in *Planned Parenthood v. Casey*: "These matters, including the most intimate and personal choices a person may make in a lifetime, choices central to personal dignity and autonomy, are central to the liberty protected by the Fourteenth Amendment. At the heart of liberty is the right to define one's own concept of existence, of meaning, of the universe, and of the mystery of human life. Beliefs about these matters could not define the attributes of personhood were they formed under compulsion of the State."

The district court analogized the "terminally ill person's choice to commit suicide" to the choice of abortion protected by *Casey*, stating: "this court finds the reasoning in *Casey* highly instructive and almost prescriptive." Like the abortion decision, the court found the decision by a terminally ill person to end his or her life to be one of the most intimate and personal that could be made in a lifetime and a choice central to personal autonomy and dignity.

The district court also found *Cruzan v. Director, Missouri Dept. of Health* to be "instructive." It quoted that case's reference to "the recognition of a general liberty interest in refusing medical treatment," and the assumption for purposes of the decision in *Cruzan* "that the United States Constitution would grant a competent person a constitutionally protected right to refuse lifesaving hydration and nutrition." The district court stated that it did not believe that a distinction of constitutional significance could be drawn "between refusing life-sustaining medical treatment and physician-assisted suicide by an uncoerced, mentally competent, terminally ill adult." Combining its exegesis of *Casey* and *Cruzan*, the district court reached its conclusion that there was a constitutional right to physician-assisted suicide.

. . . . The district court declared that there was "no question" that the "total ban" on physician-assisted suicide for the terminally ill was "an undue burden" on the constitutional right that the district court had discovered. Consequently, the statute was invalid.

Secondly, the district court held that the statute violated the Equal Protection Clause of the Fourteenth Amendment, requiring that all similarly situated persons be treated alike. Washington law, enacted in 1992, provides: "Any adult person may execute a directive directing the withholding or withdrawal of life-sustaining treatment in a terminal condition or permanent unconscious condition." Any physician who participates in good faith "in the withholding or withdrawal of life-sustaining treatment" in accordance with such a directive is immune from civil or criminal or professional liability. The district court could see no constitutional distinction between the terminally ill able to direct the withdrawal or withholding of life support and the terminally ill seeking medical aid to end their lives. Accordingly, it found an unequal application of the laws.

Washington appeals.

The conclusion of the district court that the statute deprived the plaintiffs of a liberty protected by the Fourteenth Amendment and denied them the equal protection of the laws cannot be sustained.

First. The language taken from *Casey*, on which the district court pitched its principal argument, should not be removed from the context in which it was uttered. Any reader of judicial opinions knows they often attempt a generality of expression and a sententiousness of phrase that extend far beyond the problem addressed. It is commonly accounted an error to lift sentences or even paragraphs out of one context and insert the abstracted thought into a wholly different context. To take three sentences out of an opinion over thirty pages in length dealing with the highly charged subject of abortion and to find these sentences "almost prescriptive" in ruling on a statute proscribing the promotion of suicide is to make an enormous leap, to do violence to the context, and to ignore the differences between the regulation of reproduction and the prevention of the promotion of killing a patient at his or her request.

The inappropriateness of the language of *Casey* in the situation of assisted suicide is confirmed by considering what this language, as applied by the district court, implies. The decision to choose death, according to the district court's use of *Casey*'s terms, involves "personal dignity and autonomy" and "the right to define one's own concept of existence, of meaning, of the universe, and of the mystery of human life." The district court attempted to tie these concepts to the decision of a person terminally ill. But there is no way of doing so. The category created is inherently unstable. The depressed twenty-one year old, the romantically-devastated twenty-eight year old, the alcoholic forty year old who choose suicide are also expressing their views of the existence, meaning, the universe, and life; they are also asserting their personal liberty. If at the heart of the liberty protected by the Fourteenth Amendment is this uncurtailable ability to believe and to act on one's deepest beliefs about life, the right to suicide and the right to assistance in suicide are the prerogative of at least every sane adult. The attempt to restrict such rights to the terminally ill is illusory. If such liberty exists in this context, as *Casey* asserted in the context of reproductive rights, every man and woman in the United States must enjoy it. The conclusion is a *reductio ad absurdum* [absurd].

Second. While *Casey* was not about suicide at all, *Cruzan* was about the termination of life. The district court found itself unable to distinguish between a patient refusing life support and a patient seeking medical help to bring about death and therefore interpreted *Cruzan*'s limited acknowledgment of a right to refuse treatment as tantamount to an acceptance of a terminally ill patient's right to aid in self-killing. The district court ignored the far more relevant part of the opinion in *Cruzan* that "there can be no gainsaying" a state's interest "in the protection and preservation of human life" and, as evidence of that legitimate concern, the fact that "the majority of States in this country have laws imposing criminal penalties on one who assists another to commit suicide." Whatever difficulty the district court experienced in distinguishing one situation from the other, it was not experienced by the majority in *Cruzan*.

Third. Unsupported by the gloss on "liberty" written by *Casey*, a gloss on a gloss, inasmuch as *Casey* developed an interpretation of "liberty" first elaborated in *Eisenstadt v. Baird*, and implicitly controverted by *Cruzan*, the decision of the district court lacks foundation in recent precedent. It also lacks foundation in the traditions of our nation. In the two hundred and five years of our existence no constitutional right to aid in killing oneself has ever been asserted and upheld by a court of final jurisdiction. Unless the federal judiciary is to be a floating constitutional convention, a federal court should not invent a constitutional right unknown to the past and antithetical to the defense of human life that has been a chief responsibility of our constitutional government.

Fourth. The district court extrapolated from *Casey* to hold the statute invalid on its face. That extrapolation, like the quotation from *Casey*, was an unwarranted extension of abortion jurisprudence, often unique, to a very different field. The normal rule - the rule that governs here - is that a facial challenge to a statute "must establish that no set of circumstances exists under which the Act would be valid." The district court indeed conceded that there were circumstances in which the statute could operate constitutionally, for example to deter suicide by teenagers or to prevent fraud upon the elderly. The district court did not even attempt the calculation carried out in *Casey* to show that in "a large fraction of the cases" the statute would operate un-constitutionally. From the declarations before it the district court had at most the opinion of several physicians that they "occasionally" met persons whom the statute affected detrimentally and their recitation of five case histories. There was no effort made to compare this number with the number of persons whose lives were guarded by the statute. The facial invalidation of the statute was wholly unwarranted.

Fifth. The district court declared the statute unconstitutional on its face without adequate consideration of Washington's interests that, individually and convergently, outweigh any alleged liberty of suicide. The most comprehensive study of our subject by a governmental body is *When Death Is Sought: Assisted Suicide and Euthanasia in the Medical Context*. The study was conducted by the New York State Task Force, a commission appointed by Governor Cuomo in 1985, which filed its report in May, 1994. The Task Force was composed of twenty-four members representing a broad spectrum of ethical and religious views and ethical, health, legal, and medical competencies. Its membership disagreed on the morality of suicide. Unanimously the members agreed against recommending a change in New York law to permit assisted suicide. Washington's interest in preventing such suicides is as strong as the interests that moved this diverse commission to its unanimous conclusion. A Michigan commission, set up in 1992, by majority vote in June 1994 recommended legislative change in the Michigan law against assisted suicide and set out a proposed new statute as a legislative option; the commission did not challenge the constitutionality of the existing Michigan legislation. Neither the New York nor the Michigan reports were available to the district court. We take them into account on this appeal as we take into account the legal and medical articles cited by the parties and amici [friends of the court] as representative professional judgments in this area of law. In the light of all these materials, Washington's interests are at least these:

1. The interest in not having physicians in the role of killers of their patients. "Physician-assisted suicide is fundamentally incompatible with the physician's role as healer," declares the American Medical Association's *Code of Medical Ethics*. From the Hippocratic Oath with its promise "to do no harm," to the AMA's code, the ethics of the medical profession have proscribed killing. Washington has an interest in preserving the integrity of the physician's practice as understood by physicians.

Not only would the self-understanding of physicians be affected by removal of the state's support for their professional stance; the physician's constant search for ways to combat disease would be affected, if killing were as acceptable an option for the physician as curing. The physician's commitment to curing is the medical profession's commitment to medical progress. Medically-assisted suicide as an acceptable alternative is a blind alley; Washington has a stake in barring it.

2. The interest in not subjecting the elderly and even the not-elderly but infirm to psychological pressure to consent to their own deaths. For all medical treatments, physicians decide which patients are the candidates. If assisted suicide was acceptable professional practice, physicians would make a judgment as to who was a good candidate for it. Physician neutrality and patient autonomy, independent of their physician's advice, are largely myths. Most patients do what their doctors recommend. As an eminent commission concluded, "Once the physician suggests suicide or euthanasia, some patients will feel that they have few, if any al-

ternatives, but to accept the recommendation." Washington has an interest in preventing such persuasion.

3. The interest in protecting the poor and minorities from exploitation. The poor and minorities would be especially open to manipulation in a regime of assisted suicide for two reasons: Pain is a significant factor in creating a desire for assisted suicide, and the poor and minorities are notoriously less provided for in the alleviation of pain. The desire to reduce the cost of public assistance by quickly terminating a prolonged illness cannot be ignored: "the cost of treatment is viewed as relevant to decisions at the bedside." Convergently, the reduction of untreated (although treatable) pain and economic logic would make the poorest the primest candidates for physician-assisted and physician-recommended suicide.

4. The interest in protecting all of the handicapped from societal indifference and antipathy. Among the many briefs we have received from amici curiae [friends of the court], there is one on behalf of numerous residents of nursing homes and long-term care facilities. The vulnerability of such persons to physician-assisted suicide is foreshadowed in the discriminatory way that a seriously-disabled person's expression of a desire to die is interpreted. When the non-disabled say they want to die, they are labelled as suicidal; if they are disabled, it is treated as "natural" or "reasonable." In the climate of our achievement-oriented society, "simply offering the option of 'self-deliverance' shifts a burden of proof, so that helpless patients musk ask themselves why they are not availing themselves of it." An insidious bias against the handicapped - again coupled with a cost-saving mentality - makes them especially in need of Washington's statutory protection.

An interest in preventing abuse similar to what has occurred in the Netherlands where, since 1984, legal guidelines have tacitly allowed assisted suicide or euthanasia in response to a repeated request from a suffering, competent patient. In 1990, approximately 1.8 per cent of all deaths resulted from this practice. At least an additional .8 percent of all deaths, and arguably more, come from direct measures taken to end the person's life without a contemporaneous request to end it.

Sixth. The scope of the district court's judgment is, perhaps necessarily, indefinite. The judgment of the district court was entered in favor of Jane Roe and John Doe although they were dead. This unheard-of judgment was a nullity. The judgment in favor of James Poe lapsed with his death pending appeal. The judgment in favor of Doctors Glucksberg, Halperin, Preston and Shalit was "insofar as they raise claims on behalf of their terminally ill patients." No such patients were identified by these doctors except patients who were already deceased. Presumably, then, the judgment was [on] behalf of terminally ill patients that these doctors might encounter in the future. The term "terminally ill" was not defined by the court. No class was certified by the court. There is a good deal of uncertainty on whose behalf the judgment was entered.

It was suggested in argument that a definition of the terminally ill could be supplied from the Washington statute on the refusal of life-sustaining treatment which does define "terminal condition." There are three difficulties: "terminal condition" and "terminally ill" are different terms; the examples given by the plaintiffs show considerable variation in whom they considered terminally ill to be; there is wide disagreement in definition of the terminally ill among the states. Life itself is a terminal condition, unless terminal condition is otherwise defined by a specific statute. A ter-

minal illness can vary from a sickness causing death in days
or weeks to cancer, which Dr. Glucksberg notes is "very
slow" in its deadly impact, to a heart condition which Dr.
Preston notes can be relieved by a transplant, to AIDS,
which Dr. Shalit declares is fatal once contracted. One can
only guess which definition of the terminally ill would satisfy the constitutional criteria of the district court. Consequently, an amorphous class of beneficiaries has been created in this non-class action; and the district court has
mandated Washington to reform its law against the promotion of suicide to safeguard the constitutional rights of
persons whom the district court has not identified.

Seventh. At the heart of the district court's decision appears to be its refusal to distinguish between actions taking
life and actions by which life is not supported or ceases to
be supported. This refusal undergirds the district court's
reading of *Cruzan* as well as its holding that the statute violates equal protection. The distinction, being drawn by the
legislature not on the basis of race, gender or religion or
membership in any protected class and not infringing any
fundamental constitutional right, must be upheld unless the
plaintiffs can show "that the legislature's actions were irrational." The plaintiffs have not sustained this burden.

Against the broad background of moral experience that
everyone acquires, the law of torts [civil offenses] and the
law of criminal offenses against the person have developed.
"At common law, even the touching of one person by another without consent and without legal justification was a
battery." The physician's medical expertness is not a license to inflict medical procedures against your will. Protected by the law of torts, you can have or reject such
medical treatment as you see fit. You can be left alone if
you want. Privacy in the primordial sense in which it en-

tered constitutional parlance - "the right to be let alone" -
is yours.

Tort law and criminal law have never recognized a right to
let others enslave you, mutilate you, or kill you. When you
assert a claim that another - and especially another licensed
by the state - should help you bring about your death, you
ask for more than being let alone; you ask that the state, in
protecting its own interest, not prevent its licensee from
killing. The difference is not of degree but of kind. You no
longer seek the ending of unwanted medical attention. You
seek the right to have a second person collaborate in your
death. To protect all the interests enumerated under
"Fifth" above, the statute rightly and reasonably draws the
line.

Compassion, according to the reflections of Prince
Myshkin [in Feodor Dostoevsky's *The Idiot*], is "the most
important, perhaps the sole law of human existence." In
the vernacular, compassion is trumps. No one can read the
accounts of the sufferings of the deceased plaintiffs supplied by their declarations, or the accounts of the sufferings
of their patients supplied by the physicians, without being
moved by them. No one would inflict such sufferings on
another or want them inflicted on himself; and since the
horrors recounted are those that could attend the end of
life anyone who reads of them must be aware that they
could be attendant on his own death. The desire to have a
good and kind way of forestalling them is understandably
evident in the declarations of the plaintiffs and in the decision of the district court.

Compassion is a proper, desirable, even necessary component of judicial character, but compassion is not the most
important, certainly not the sole law of human existence.
Unrestrained by other virtues, as *The Idiot* illustrates, it leads

to catastrophe. Justice, prudence, and fortitude are necessary too. Compassion cannot be the compass of a federal judge. That compass is the Constitution of the United States. Where, as here in the case of Washington, the statute of a state comports with that compass, the validity of the statute must be upheld.

For all the foregoing reasons, the judgment appealed from [the District Court] is reversed.

Compassion in Dying v. Washington State
March 6, 1996

Circuit Judge Stephen Reinhardt: This case raises an extraordinarily important and difficult issue. It compels us to address questions to which there are no easy or simple answers, at law or otherwise. It requires us to confront the most basic of human concerns - the mortality of self and loved ones - and to balance the interest in preserving human life against the desire to die peacefully and with dignity. People of good will can and do passionately disagree about the proper result, perhaps even more intensely than they part ways over the constitutionality of restricting a woman's right to have an abortion. Heated though the debate may be, we must determine whether and how the United States Constitution applies to the controversy before us, a controversy that may touch more people more profoundly than any other issue the courts will face in the foreseeable future.

Today, we are required to decide whether a person who is terminally ill has a constitutionally-protected liberty interest in hastening what might otherwise be a protracted, undignified, and extremely painful death. If such an interest exists, we must next decide whether or not the state of Washington may constitutionally restrict its exercise by banning a form of medical assistance that is frequently requested by terminally ill people who wish to die. We first conclude that there is a constitutionally-protected liberty interest in determining the time and manner of one's own death, an interest that must be weighed against the state's legitimate and countervailing interests, especially those that relate to the preservation of human life. After balancing the competing interests, we conclude by answering the narrow question before us: We hold that insofar as the Washington statute prohibits physicians from prescribing life-ending medication for use by terminally ill, competent adults who wish to hasten their own deaths, it violates the Due Process Clause of the Fourteenth Amendment.

This is the first right-to-die case that this court or any other federal court of appeals has ever decided. The plaintiffs are four physicians who treat terminally ill patients, three terminally ill patients, and a Washington non-profit organization called Compassion In Dying. The four physicians - Dr. Harold Glucksberg, Dr. Thomas A. Preston, Dr. Abigail Halperin, and Dr. Peter Shalit - are respected doctors whose expertise is recognized by the state. All declare that they periodically treat terminally ill, competent adults who wish to hasten their deaths with help from their physicians. The doctors state that in their professional judgment they should provide that help but are deterred from doing so by a Washington statute that makes it a felony to knowingly aid another person to commit suicide.

Under the Washington statute, aiding a person who wishes to end his life constitutes a criminal act and subjects the aider to the possibility of a lengthy term of imprisonment, even if the recipient of the aid is a terminally ill, competent adult and the aider is a licensed physician who is providing medical assistance at the request of the patient. The Washington statute provides in pertinent part: "A person is guilty of promoting a suicide when he knowingly causes or aids another person to attempt suicide." A violation of the statute constitutes a felony punishable by imprisonment for a maximum of five years and a fine of up to $10,000.

On appeal, the four plaintiff-doctors asserted the rights of terminally ill, competent adult patients who wished to hasten their deaths with the help of their physicians so that they might die peacefully and with dignity. That group included the three patient-plaintiffs. The district court described the patient-plaintiffs, each of whom desired to obtain prescription drugs to hasten his death, as follows:

Jane Roe is a 69-year-old retired pediatrician who has suffered since 1988 from cancer which has now metastasized throughout her skeleton. Although she tried and benefited temporarily from various treatments including chemotherapy and radiation, she is now in the terminal phase of her disease. In November 1993, her doctor referred her to hospice care. Only patients with a life expectancy of less than six months are eligible for such care.

Jane Roe has been almost completely bedridden since June of 1993 and experiences constant pain, which becomes especially sharp and severe when she moves. The only medical treatment available to her at this time is medication, which cannot fully alleviate her pain. In addition, she suffers from swollen legs, bed sores, poor appetite, nausea and vomiting, impaired vision, incontinence of bowel, and general weakness.

Jane Roe is mentally competent and wishes to hasten her death by taking prescribed drugs with the help of plaintiff Compassion in Dying. In keeping with the requirements of that organization, she has made three requests for its members to provide her and her family with counseling, emotional support, and any necessary ancillary drug assistance at the time she takes the drugs.

John Doe is a 44-year-old artist dying of AIDS. Since his diagnosis in 1991, he has experienced two bouts of pneumonia, chronic, severe skin and sinus infections, grand mal seizures and extreme fatigue. He has already lost 70% of his vision to cytomegalovirus retinitis, a degenerative disease which will result in blindness and rob him of his ability to paint. His doctor has indicated that he is in the terminal phase of his illness.

John Doe is especially cognizant of the suffering imposed by a lingering terminal illness because he was the primary caregiver for his long-term companion who died of AIDS in June of 1991. He also observed his grandfather's death from diabetes preceded by multiple amputations as well as loss of vision and hearing. Mr. Doe is mentally competent, understands there is no cure for AIDS and wants his physician to prescribe drugs which he can use to hasten his death.

James Poe is a 69-year-old retired sales representative who suffers from emphysema, which causes him a constant sensation of suffocating. He is connected to an oxygen tank at all times, and takes morphine regularly to calm the panic reaction associated with his feeling of suffocation. Mr. Poe also suffers from heart failure related to his pulmonary disease which obstructs the flow of blood to his extremities and causes severe leg pain. There are no cures for his pulmonary and cardiac conditions, and he is in the terminal phase of his illness. Mr. Poe is mentally competent and wishes to commit suicide by taking physician-prescribed drugs.

The names of the patients are pseudonymous in order to protect their privacy. All three patients died after the case began. Two had died by the time the District Court issued its decision. The other died prior to the date of the decision by the three-judge panel of this court.

Since the District Court properly granted the physicians standing [the right] to assert the rights of their terminally ill patients in general, it is clear that this case was not rendered moot by the death of the three named patients. . . .

The doctors here also meet the standing requirements because they run a severe risk of prosecution under the Washington statute, which proscribes the very conduct in which they seek to engage. The state has never indicated that it would not prosecute doctors who violate that law.

We need not decide whether, the deaths of the three patient-plaintiffs would negate the ability of their lawyers to continue the challenge that those patients brought while they were still alive. . . .

The District Court in this case reached only claims asserted by two of the three categories of plaintiffs: the patients' claims that they had a right to receive medical assistance from their physicians and the claims that the physicians asserted on behalf of their patients. It did not address the claim asserted by Compassion In Dying. Nor, correlatively, did it reach the claim by the terminally ill patients that they had a right to receive assistance from organizations such as Compassion In Dying.

Like the District Court, we decide only claims brought by the terminally ill patients and the doctors. We consider those claims to the extent that they relate to the provision of certain medical assistance to terminally ill persons by physicians or persons acting pursuant to their authorization or direction. The claims involving Compassion In Dying are not before us. The district court suggested that it would reach those additional claims at a later stage in the proceedings if Compassion In Dying so desired. . . .

The plaintiffs do not challenge [the] Washington statute [prohibiting physician-assisted suicide] in its entirety. Specifically they do not object to the portion of the Washington statute that makes it unlawful for a person knowingly to *cause* another to commit suicide. Rather, they only challenge the statute's *"or aids"* provision. They challenge that provision both on its face and as applied to terminally ill, mentally competent adults who wish to hasten their own deaths with the help of medication prescribed by their doctors. The plaintiffs contend that the provision impermissibly prevents the exercise by terminally ill patients of a constitutionally-protected liberty interest in violation of the Due Process Clause of the Fourteenth Amendment, and also that it impermissibly distinguishes between similarly situated terminally ill patients in violation of the Equal Protection Clause.

In an extremely thoughtful opinion, Chief District Judge Barbara Rothstein held that "a competent, terminally ill adult has a constitutionally guaranteed right under the Fourteenth Amendment to commit physician-assisted suicide." . . . [T]he District Court concluded that the Washington statute places an undue burden on the exercise of that constitutionally-protected liberty interest. The District Court held that the Washington law also violates the Equal Protection Clause because it impermissibly treats similarly situated groups of terminally ill patients differently. Although the scope of the relief the District Judge ordered is not clear, it appears that she declared the statute invalid only insofar as it applies to the prescription of medication to terminally ill competent adults who wish to hasten their deaths - or, to use the district court's precise terminology, only insofar as it applies to "physician-assisted suicide."

On appeal, a three-judge panel of this court voted 2-1 to reverse the district court decision. The majority held that there is no due process liberty interest in physician-assisted suicide. It also concluded that the Washington statute does not violate the Equal Protection Clause. Accordingly, the majority held that the statute is not invalid facially or as applied. . . . Because of the extraordinary importance of this case, we decided to rehear it en banc [with the entire court participating in the decision].

We now affirm the District Court's decision and clarify the scope of the relief. We hold that the "or aids" provision of [the] Washington statute [prohibiting physician-assisted suicide] as applied to the prescription of life-ending medication for use by terminally ill, competent adult patients who wish to hasten their deaths, violates the Due Process Clause of the Fourteenth Amendment. Accordingly, we need not resolve the question whether that provision, in conjunction with other Washington laws regulating the treatment of terminally ill patients, also violates the Equal Protection Clause.

In order to answer the question whether the Washington statute violates the Due Process Clause insofar as it prohibits the provision of certain medical assistance to terminally ill, competent adults who wish to hasten their own deaths, we first determine whether there is a liberty interest in choosing the time and manner of one's death - a question sometimes phrased in common parlance as: Is there a right to die? Because we hold that there is, we must then determine whether prohibiting physicians from prescribing life-ending medication for use by terminally ill patients who wish to die violates the patients' due process rights.

The mere recognition of a liberty interest does not mean that a state may not prohibit the exercise of that interest in particular circumstances, nor does it mean that a state may not adopt appropriate regulations governing its exercise. Rather, in cases like the one before us, the courts must apply a balancing test under which we weigh the individual's liberty interests against the relevant state interests in order to determine whether the state's actions are constitutionally permissible. As Chief Justice Rehnquist, writing for the Court, explained in *Cruzan*, the only right-to-die case that the Court has heretofore considered:

> [D]etermining that a person has a "liberty interest" under the Due Process Clause does not end our inquiry; "whether respondent's constitutional rights have been violated must be determined by balancing his liberty interests against the relevant state interests."

. . . . As Justice O'Connor explained in her concurring opinion in *Cruzan*, the ultimate question is whether sufficient justification exists for the intrusion by the government into the realm of a person's "liberty, dignity, and freedom." If the balance favors the state, then the given statute - whether it regulates the exercise of a due process liberty interest or prohibits that exercise to some degree - is constitutional. If the balance favors the individual, then the statute - whatever its justifications - violates the individual's due process liberty rights and must be declared unconstitutional, either on its face or as applied. Here, we conclude unhesitatingly that the balance favors the individual's liberty interest.

Before beginning our inquiry into whether a liberty interest exists, we reiterate a few fundamental precepts that guide us. The first lies in the Court's cautionary note in *Roe v. Wade*:

We forthwith acknowledge our awareness of the sensitive and emotional nature of the . . . controversy, of the vigorous opposing views, even among physicians, and of the deep and seemingly absolute convictions that the subject inspires. One's philosophy, one's experiences, one's exposure to the raw edges of human existence, one's religious training, one's attitude toward life and family and their values, and the moral standards one establishes and seeks to observe, are all likely to influence and to color one's thinking and conclusions. . . .

Like the *Roe* Court, we endeavor to conduct an objective analysis of a most emotionally-charged of topics. In doing so, we bear in mind the second Justice Harlan's admonition in his now-vindicated dissent in *Poe v. Ullman*:

[T]he full scope of the liberty guaranteed by the Due Process Clause cannot be found in or limited by the precise terms of the specific guarantees elsewhere in the Constitution. This 'liberty' is not a series of isolated points pricked out in terms of the taking of property; the freedom of speech, press, and religion; the right to keep and bear arms; the freedom from unreasonable searches and seizures; and so on. It is a rational continuum which, broadly speaking, includes a freedom from all substantial arbitrary impositions and purposeless restraints, . . . and which also recognizes, what a reasonable and sensitive judgment must, that certain interests require particularly careful scrutiny of the state needs asserted to justify their abridgment.

Applying Justice Harlan's teaching, we must strive to resist the natural judicial impulse to limit our vision to that which can plainly be observed on the face of the document before us, or even that which we have previously had the wisdom to recognize.

Most important, we undertake our difficult task with a profound respect for the noble objectives of the Constitution, as described by Justice Brandeis in the second most famous dissent in American jurisprudence. In *Olmstead v. United States*, Justice Brandeis wrote, and his words have since been quoted in full in several opinions of the Court and in innumerable appellate court decisions:

> The makers of our Constitution undertook to secure conditions favorable to the pursuit of happiness. They recognized the significance of man's spiritual nature, of his feelings and of his intellect. They knew that only a part of the pain, pleasure and satisfaction of life are to be found in material things. They sought to protect Americans in their beliefs, their thoughts, their emotions and their sensations. They conferred, as against the government, the right to be let alone - the most comprehensive of rights, and the right most valued by civilized men.

In examining whether a liberty interest exists in determining the time and manner of one's death, we begin with the compelling similarities between right-to-die cases and abortion cases. In the former as in the latter, the relative strength of the competing interests changes as physical, medical, or related circumstances vary. In right-to-die cases the outcome of the balancing test may differ at different points along the life cycle as a person's physical or medical condition deteriorates, just as in abortion cases the permissibility of restrictive state legislation may vary with the progression of the pregnancy. Equally important, both types of cases raise issues of life and death, and both arouse similar religious and moral concerns. Both also present basic questions about an individual's right of choice.

Historical evidence shows that both abortion and assisted suicide were for many years condemned, but that the efforts to prevent people from engaging in the condemned conduct were always at most only partially successful. Even when prohibited, abortions and assisted-suicides flourished in back alleys, in small street-side clinics, and in the privacy of the bedroom. Deprived of the right to medical assistance, many pregnant women and terminally ill adults ultimately took matters into their own hands, often with tragic consequences.

Because they present issues of such profound spiritual importance and because they so deeply affect individuals' right to determine their own destiny, the abortion and right-to-die cases have given rise to a highly emotional and divisive debate. In many respects, the legal arguments on both sides are similar, as are the constitutional principles at issue.

In deciding right-to-die cases, we are guided by the Court's approach to the abortion cases. *Casey* in particular provides a powerful precedent, for in that case the Court had the opportunity to evaluate its past decisions and to determine whether to adhere to its original judgment. Although *Casey* was influenced by the doctrine of stare decisis [letting previous decisions stand], the fundamental message of that case lies in its statements regarding the type of issue that confronts us here: "These matters, involving the most intimate and personal choices a person may make in a lifetime, choices central to personal dignity and autonomy, are central to the liberty protected by the Fourteenth Amendment."

The majority opinion of the three-judge panel that first heard this case on appeal defined the claimed liberty interest as a "constitutional right to *aid* in killing oneself." However, the subject we must initially examine is not nearly so limited. Properly analyzed, the first issue to be resolved is whether there is a liberty interest in determining the time and manner of one's death. We do not ask simply whether there is a liberty interest in receiving "aid in killing oneself" because such a narrow interest could not exist in the absence of a broader and more important underlying interest - the right to die. In short, it is the end and not the means that defines the liberty interest.

The broader approach we employ in defining the liberty interest is identical to the approach used by the Supreme Court in the abortion cases. In those cases, the Court initially determined whether a general liberty interest existed (an interest in having an abortion), not whether there was an interest in implementing that general liberty interest by a particular means (with medical assistance). Specifically, in *Roe v. Wade*, the Court determined that women had a liberty interest in securing an abortion, not that women had a liberty interest in obtaining medical assistance for purpose of an abortion. The Court did so even though the Texas statute at issue did not prohibit a woman from inducing her own abortion; nor did it criminalize a woman's conduct in securing an abortion. Rather, the Texas statute, like the Washington statute here, prohibited the rendering of assistance; specifically, the Texas statute prohibited only *assisting* a woman to secure an abortion. The Court first determined that a woman had a constitutional right to choose an abortion. Only after it did so, did it proceed to the second step: to determine whether the state's prohibition on assistance unconstitutionally restricted the exercise of that liberty interest. Similarly, in *Planned Parenthood v. Casey* the Court first reaffirmed, after extensive analysis, its earlier holding that women have a liberty interest in obtaining an abortion. In determining the *existence* of that liberty interest, the Court did not address the subject of spousal notification. As in *Roe*, only after affirming a woman's right to have an abortion, did the Court proceed to the second step: to examine whether the statutory provision requiring married women to notify their spouses prior to obtaining an abortion posed an undue burden on the exercise of that liberty interest. In this case, our analysis is necessarily the same. First we must determine whether there *is* a liberty interest in determining the time and manner of one's death; if so, we must then examine whether Washington's ban on assisted suicide unconstitutionally restricts the exercise of that liberty interest.

While some people refer to the liberty interest implicated in right-to-die cases as a liberty interest in committing suicide, we do not describe it that way. We use the broader and more accurate terms, "the right to die," "determining the time and manner of one's death," and "hastening one's death" for an important reason. The liberty interest we examine encompasses a whole range of acts that are generally not considered to constitute "suicide." Included within the liberty interest we examine, is for example, the act of refusing or terminating unwanted medical treatment. As we discuss later, a competent adult has a liberty interest in refusing to be connected to a respirator or in being disconnected from one, even if he is terminally ill and cannot live without mechanical assistance. The law does not classify the death of a patient that results from the granting of his wish to decline or discontinue treatment as "suicide." Nor does the law label the acts of those who help the patient carry out that wish, whether by physically disconnecting the respirator or by removing an intravenous tube, as assistance in suicide. Accordingly, we believe that the broader terms - "the right to die," "controlling the time and manner of one's death," and "hastening one's death" - more accurately describe the liberty interest at issue here. Moreover, as we discuss later, we have serious doubts that the terms "suicide" and "assisted suicide" are appropriate legal descriptions of the specific conduct at issue here.

There is one further definitional matter we should emphasize. Following our determination regarding the existence of a liberty interest in hastening one's death, we examine whether the Washington statute unconstitutionally infringes on that liberty interest. Throughout that examination, we use the term "physician-assisted suicide," a term that does not appear in the Washington statute but is frequently employed in legal and medical discussions involving the type of question before us. For purposes of this opinion, we use physician-assisted suicide as it is used by the parties and district court and as it is most frequently used: the prescribing of medication by a physician for the purpose of enabling a patient to end his life. It is only that conduct that the plaintiffs urge be held constitutionally-protected in this case.

There is no litmus test for courts to apply when deciding whether or not a liberty interest exists under the Due Process Clause. Our decisions involve difficult judgments regarding the conscience, traditions, and fundamental tenets of our nation. We must sometimes apply those basic principles in light of changing values based on shared experience. Other times we must apply them to new problems arising out of the development and use of new technologies. In all cases, our analysis of the applicability of the protections of the Constitution must be made in light of existing circumstances as well as our historic traditions.

Historically, the Court has classified "fundamental rights" as those that are "implicit in the concept of ordered liberty." The Court reasserted this historic standard, along with an alternative description, in its highly controversial *Bowers v. Hardwick* opinion:

> Striving to assure itself and the public that announcing rights not readily identifiable in the Constitution's text involves much more than the imposition of the Justices' own choice of values on the States and the Federal Government, the Court has sought to identify the nature of the rights qualifying for heightened judicial protection. In *Palko v. Connecticut*, it was said that this category includes those fundamental liberties that are "implicit in the concept of ordered liberty," such that "neither liberty nor justice would exist if [they] were sacrificed." A different description of fundamental liberties appeared in *Moore v. East Cleveland*, where they are characterized as those liberties that are "deeply rooted in this Nation's history and tradition."

In recent years, the Court has spoken more frequently of substantive due process *interests* than of *fundamental* due process *rights*. The Court has also recently expressed a strong reluctance to find new fundamental rights.

The Court's evolving doctrinal approach to substantive due process claims is consistent with the basic truth enunciated by Justice Harlan and later endorsed by the Court in *Casey*: "the full scope of the liberty guaranteed by the Due Process Clause is a rational continuum which, broadly speaking, includes a freedom from all substantial arbitrary impositions and purposeless restraints . . ." . As Justice Harlan noted, some liberty interests are weightier than others. Under the

Court's traditional jurisprudence, those classified as fundamental rights cannot be limited except to further a compelling and narrowly tailored state interest. Other important interests, such as the liberty interest in refusing unwanted medical treatment, are subject to a balancing test that is less restrictive, but nonetheless requires the state to overcome a substantial hurdle in justifying any significant impairment.

Recent cases, including *Cruzan*, suggest that the Court may be heading towards the formal adoption of the continuum approach, along with a balancing test, in substantive due process cases generally. If so, there would no longer be a two-tier or three-tier set of tests that depends on the classification of the right or interest as fundamental, important, or marginal. Instead, the more important the individual's right or interest, the more persuasive the justifications for infringement would have to be. We see the evolution in the Court's approach more as a recognition of the artificiality of the current classification system than as a fundamental change in the Court's practical approach to specific issues. So long as the liberty interest is an important one, the state must shoulder the burden of justifying any significant limitations it seeks to impose. However, we need not predict the Court's future course in order to decide the case before us. Here, as we have said, even under the Court's traditional mode of analysis, a balancing test is applicable.

. . . . Although in determining the existence of important rights or liberty interests, the Court examines our history and experience, it has stated on a number of occasions that the limits of the substantive reach of the Due Process Clause are not frozen at any point in time. In *Casey*, the Court said: "Neither the Bill of Rights nor the specific practices of States at the time of the adoption of the Fourteenth Amendment marks the outer limits of the substantive sphere of liberty which the Fourteenth Amendment protects." Justice Frankfurter may have put it best when, writing for the Court in *Rochin v. California,* he declared, "To believe that this judicial exercise of judgment could be avoided by freezing 'due process of law' at some fixed stage in time or thought is to suggest that the most important aspect of constitutional adjudication is a function for in-animate machines and not for judges . . . ." Certainly, it would be difficult to imagine a more felicitous expression of the dynamism of constitutional interpretation. Thus, while historical analysis plays a useful role in any attempt to de-termine whether a claimed right or liberty interest exists, earlier legislative or judicial recognition of the right or inter-est is not a *sine qua non* [given].

In *Casey,* the Court made it clear that the fact that we have previously failed to acknowledge the existence of a particu-lar liberty interest or even that we have previously prohib-ited its exercise is no barrier to recognizing its existence. In discussing a woman's liberty interest in securing an abor-tion, the *Casey* Court stated that pregnancy involves "suffering [that] is too intimate and personal for the State to insist, without more, upon its own vision of the woman's role, *however dominant that vision has been in the course of our his-tory and culture.*"

In contrast to *Casey,* the majority opinion of the three-judge panel in the case now before us erroneously concluded that a historical analysis alone is sufficient basis for rejecting plaintiffs' claim to a substantive liberty interest or right. As explained below, we believe that the panel's historical ac-count is misguided, but even if it were indisputably correct, historical evidence alone is not a sufficient basis for reject-ing a claimed liberty interest.

Were history our sole guide, the Virginia anti-miscegenation statute that the Court unanimously overturned in *Loving v.*

Virginia as violative of substantive due process and the Equal Protection Clause, would still be in force because such anti-miscegenation laws were commonplace both when the United States was founded and when the Fourteenth Amendment was adopted. The Court explicitly acknowledged as much in *Casey*, in rejecting the view that substantive due process protects rights or liberties only if they possess a historical pedigree. In *Casey*, the Court said:

> It is . . . tempting . . . to suppose that the Due Process Clause protects only those practices, defined at the most specific level, that were protected against government interference by other rules of law when the Fourteenth Amendment was ratified. . . . But such a view would be inconsistent with our law. It is a promise of the Constitution that there is a realm of personal liberty which the government may not enter. We have vindicated this principle before. Marriage is mentioned nowhere in the Bill of Rights and interracial marriage was illegal in most States in the 19th century, but the Court was no doubt correct in finding it to be an aspect of liberty protected against state interference by the substantive component of the Due Process Clause in *Loving*. . . .

Indeed, if historical evidence of accepted practices at the time the Fourteenth Amendment was enacted were dispositive, the Court would not only have decided *Loving* differently, but it would not have held that women have a right to have an abortion. As [then Associate Justice Rehnquist's] dissent pointed out in *Roe*, more than three-quarters of the existing states (at least 28 out of 37 states), as well as eight territorial legislatures restricted or prohibited abortions in 1868 when the Fourteenth Amendment was adopted.

The majority opinion of the three-judge panel claimed that "a constitutional right to aid in killing oneself" was "unknown to the past." As we have pointed out, our inquiry is not so narrow. Nor is our conclusion so facile. The relevant historical record is far more checkered than the majority would have us believe.

Like the Court in *Roe*, we begin with ancient attitudes. In Greek and Roman times, far from being universally prohibited, suicide was often considered commendable in literature, mythology, and practice.

> The first of all literary suicides, that of Oedipus' mother, Jocasta, is made to seem praiseworthy, an honorable way out of an insufferable situation. Homer records self-murder without comment, as something natural and heroic. The legends bear him out. Aegeus threw himself into the sea - which therefore bore his name - when he mistakenly thought his son Theseus had been slain by the Minotaur.

In Athens, as well as the Greek colonies of Marseilles and Ceos, magistrates kept a supply of hemlock for those who wished to end their lives. The magistrates even supplied those who wished to commit suicide with the means to do so.

> Whoever no longer wishes to live shall state his reasons to the Senate, and after having received permission shall abandon life. If your existence is hateful to you, die; if you are overwhelmed by fate, drink the hemlock. If you are bowed with grief, abandon life. Let the unhappy man recount his misfortune, let the magistrate supply him with the remedy, and his wretchedness will come to an end.

While Socrates counseled his disciples against committing suicide, he willingly drank the hemlock as he was condemned to do, and his example inspired others to end their lives. Plato, Socrates' most distinguished student, believed suicide was often justifiable.

> He suggested that if life itself became immoderate, then suicide became a rational, justifiable act. Painful disease, or intolerable constraint were sufficient reasons to depart. And this when religious superstitions faded was philosophic justification enough.

Many contemporaries of Plato were even more inclined to find suicide a legitimate and acceptable act. In *Roe*, while surveying the attitudes of the Greeks toward abortion, the Court stated that "only the Pythagorean school of philosophers frowned on the related act of suicide"; it then noted that the Pythagorean school represented a distinctly minority view.

The Stoics glorified suicide as an act of pure rational will. Cato, who killed himself to avoid dishonor when Caesar crushed his military aspirations, was the most celebrated of the many suicides among the Stoics. Montaigne wrote of Cato: "This was a man chosen by nature to show the heights which can be attained by human steadfastness and constancy. . . . Such courage is above philosophy."

Like the Greeks, the Romans often considered suicide to be acceptable or even laudable.

> To live nobly also meant to die nobly and at the right time. Everything depended on a dominant will and a rational choice.

This attitude was reinforced by Roman law. . . . According to Justinian's *Digest*, suicide of a private citizen was not punishable if it was caused by "impatience of pain or sickness, or by another cause," or by "weariness of life . . . lunacy, or fear of dishonor." Since this covered every rational cause, all that was left was the utterly irrational suicide "without cause," and that was punishable on the grounds that "whoever does not spare himself would much less spare another." In other words, it was punished because irrational, not because it was a crime.

The Romans did sometimes punish suicide. Under Roman law, people convicted of crimes forfeited their property to the Emperor, thereby disinheriting their heirs. Roman law imposed a special penalty on people who were caught committing a crime and then committed suicide prior to conviction to avoid forfeiting the property. To protect the Emperor's interests, the property of people who committed suicide under such circumstances was forfeited, just as if they had been convicted of the crime involved.

The early Christians saw death as an escape from the tribulations of a fallen existence and as the doorway to heaven. "In other words, the more powerfully the Church instilled in believers the idea that this world was a vale of tears and sin and temptation, where they waited uneasily until death released them into eternal glory, the more irresistible the temptation to suicide became." The Christian impulse to martyrdom reached its height with the Donatists, who were so eager to enter into martyrdom that they were eventually declared heretics. Gibbon, in the *Decline and Fall of the Roman Empire*, described them this way:

They sometimes forced their way into courts of justice and compelled the affrighted judge to give orders for their execution. They frequently stopped travellers on the public highways and obliged them to inflict the stroke of martyrdom by promise of a reward, if they consented - and by the threat of instant death, if they refused to grant so singular a favour.

St. Augustine said of the Donatists, "to kill themselves out of respect for martyrdom is their daily sport." Prompted in large part by the utilitarian concern that the rage for suicide would deplete the ranks of Christians, St. Augustine argued that committing suicide was a "detestable and damnable wickedness" and was able to help turn the tide of public opinion. Even staunch opponents of a constitutional right to suicide acknowledge that "there were many examples of Christian martyrs whose deaths bordered on suicide, and confusion regarding the distinction between suicide and martyrdom existed up until the time of St. Augustine (354-430 A.D.)."

In 562 A.D., the Council of Braga denied funeral rites to anyone who killed himself. A little more than a century later, in 693 A.D., the Council of Toledo declared that anyone who attempted suicide should be excommunicated. Once established, the Christian view that suicide was in all cases a sin and crime held sway for 1,000 years until philosophers, poets, and even some clergymen - Montesquieu, Voltaire, Diderot, Francis Bacon, David Hume, John Donne, Sir Thomas More, among others - began to challenge the all-encompassing nature of the dominant ideology. In his book *Utopia*, Sir Thomas More, who was later canonized by the Roman Catholic Church, strongly supported the right of the terminally ill to commit suicide and also expressed approval of the practice of assisting those who wished to hasten their deaths. Hume argued that a decision by a terminally ill patient to end his life was often laudable. France even enacted a statute legalizing suicide in 1790, primarily as a result of the influence of the nation's leading philosophers.

Suicide was a crime under the English common law [that established by custom and usage], at least in limited circumstances, probably as early as the thirteenth century. Bracton, incorporating Roman Law as set forth in Justinian's *Digest*, declared that if someone commits suicide to avoid conviction of a felony, his property escheats to his lords. Bracton said "[i]t ought to be otherwise if he kills himself through madness or unwillingness to endure suffering." Despite his general fidelity to Roman law, Bracton did introduce a key innovation: "[I]f a man slays himself in weariness of life or because he is unwilling to endure further bodily pain . . . he may have a successor, but his movable goods [personal property] are confiscated. He does not lose his inheritance [real property], only his movable goods." Bracton's innovation was incorporated into English common law, which has thus treated suicides resulting from the inability to "endure further bodily pain" with compassion and understanding ever since a common law scheme was firmly established.

Sir Edward Coke, in his *Third Institute* published in 1644, held that killing oneself was an offense and that someone who committed suicide should forfeit his movable property. But Coke listed an exception for someone who "by the rage of sickness or infirmity or otherwise," kills himself "while he is not of compos mentia," or sound mind. In eighteenth century England, many and perhaps most juries compensated for the perceived unfairness of the law by concluding that anyone who killed himself was necessarily *not* of sound mind. Thus, although, formally, suicide was long considered a crime under English common law, in practice it was a crime that was punished leniently, if at all, because juries frequently used their power to nullify the law.

The traditional English experience was also shaped by the taboos that have long colored our views of suicide and perhaps still do today. English common law reflected the ancient fear that the spirit of someone who ended his own life would return to haunt the living. Accordingly, the traditional practice was to bury the body at a crossroads - either so the suicide could not find his way home or so that the frequency of travelers would keep his spirit from rising. As added insurance, a stake was driven through the body.

English attitudes toward suicide, including the tradition of ignominious burial, carried over to America where they subsequently underwent a transformation. By 1798, six of the 13 original colonies had abolished all penalties for suicide either by statute or state constitution. There is no evidence that any court ever imposed a punishment for suicide or attempted suicide under common law in post-revolutionary America. By the time the Fourteenth Amendment was adopted in 1868, suicide was generally not punishable, and in only nine of the 37 states is it clear that there were statutes prohibiting assisting suicide.

The majority of states have not criminalized suicide or attempted suicide since the turn of the century. The New Jersey Supreme Court declared in 1901 that since suicide was not punishable it should not be considered a crime. "[A]ll will admit that in some cases it is ethically defensible," the court said, as when a woman kills herself to escape being raped or "when a man curtails weeks or months of agony of an incurable disease." Today, no state has a statute prohibiting suicide or attempted suicide; nor has any state had such a statute for at least 10 years. A majority of states do, however, still have laws on the books against assisting suicide.

Clearly the absence of a criminal sanction alone does not show societal approbation of a practice. Nor is there any evidence that Americans approve of suicide in general. In recent years, however, there has been increasingly widespread support for allowing the terminally ill to hasten their deaths and avoid painful, undignified, and inhumane endings to their lives. Most Americans simply do not appear to view such acts as constituting suicide, and there is much support in reason for that conclusion.

Polls have repeatedly shown that a large majority of Americans - sometimes nearing 90% - fully endorse recent legal changes granting terminally ill patients, and sometimes their families, the prerogative to accelerate their death by refusing or terminating treatment. Other polls indicate that a majority of Americans favor doctor-assisted suicide for the terminally ill. In April, 1990, the Roper Report found that 64% of Americans believed that the terminally ill should have the right to request and receive physician aid-in-dying. Another national poll, conducted in October 1991, shows that "nearly two out of three Americans favor doctor-assisted suicide and euthanasia for terminally ill patients who request it." A 1994 Harris poll found 73% of Americans favor legalizing physician-assisted suicide. Three states have held referenda on proposals to allow physicians to help terminally ill, competent adults commit suicide with somewhat mixed results. In Oregon, voters approved the carefully-crafted referendum by a margin of 51 to 49 percent in November of 1994. In Washington and California where the measures contained far fewer practical safeguards, they narrowly failed to pass, each drawing 46 percent of the vote. As such referenda indicate, there is unquestionably growing popular support for permitting doctors to provide assistance to terminally ill patients who wish to hasten their deaths.

Just as the mere absence of criminal statutes prohibiting suicide or attempted suicide does not indicate societal approval so the mere presence of statutes criminalizing assisting in a suicide does not necessarily indicate societal disapproval. That is especially true when such laws are seldom, if ever, enforced. There is no reported American case of criminal punishment being meted out to a doctor for helping a patient hasten his own death. The lack of enforcement of statutes prohibiting assisting a mentally competent, terminally ill adult to end his own life would appear to reflect widespread societal disaffection with such laws.

Our attitudes toward suicide of the type at issue in this case are better understood in light of our unwritten history and of technological developments. Running beneath the official history of legal condemnation of physician-assisted suicide is a strong undercurrent of a time-honored but hidden practice of physicians helping terminally ill patients to hasten their deaths. According to a survey by the American Society of Internal Medicine, one doctor in five said he had assisted in a patient's suicide. Accounts of doctors who have helped their patients end their lives have appeared both in professional journals and in the daily press.

The debate over whether terminally ill patients should have a right to reject medical treatment or to receive aid from their physicians in hastening their deaths has taken on a new prominence as a result of a number of developments. Two hundred years ago when America was founded and more than one hundred years ago when the Fourteenth Amendment was adopted, Americans died from a slew of illness and infirmities that killed their victims quickly but today are almost never fatal in this nation - scarlet fever, cholera, measles, diarrhea, influenza, pneumonia, gastritis, to name a few. Other diseases that have not been conquered can now often be controlled for years, if not decades - diseases such as diabetes, muscular dystrophy, Parkinson's disease, cardiovascular disease, and certain types of cancer. As a result, Americans are living longer, and when they finally succumb to illness, lingering longer, either in great pain or in a stuporous, semi-comatose condition that results from the infusion of vast amounts of pain killing medications. Despite the marvels of technology, Americans frequently die with less dignity than they did in the days when ravaging diseases typically ended their lives quickly. AIDS, which often subjects its victims to a horrifying and drawn-out demise, has also contributed to the growing number of terminally ill patients who die protracted and painful deaths.

One result has been a growing movement to restore humanity and dignity to the process by which Americans die. The now recognized right to refuse or terminate treatment and the emergent right to receive medical assistance in hastening one's death are inevitable consequences of changes in the causes of death, advances in medical science, and the development of new technologies. Both the need and the capability to assist individuals end their lives in peace and dignity have increased exponentially.

Next we examine previous Court decisions that delineate the boundaries of substantive due process. We believe that a careful examination of these decisions demonstrates that there is a strong liberty interest in determining how and when one's life shall end, and that an explicit recognition of that interest follows naturally, indeed inevitably, from their reasoning.

The essence of the substantive component of the Due Process Clause is to limit the ability of the state to intrude into the most important matters of our lives, at least without substantial justification. In a long line of cases, the Court has carved out certain key moments and decisions in individuals' lives and placed them beyond the general prohibitory authority of the state. The Court has recognized that the Fourteenth Amendment affords constitutional protection to personal decisions relating to marriage, procreation, family relationships, child rearing and education, and intercourse for purposes other than procreation. The Court has recognized the right of individuals to be free from government interference in deciding matters as personal as whether to bear or beget a child, and whether to continue an unwanted pregnancy to term.

A common thread running through these cases is that they involve decisions that are highly personal and intimate, as well as of great importance to the individual. Certainly, few decisions are more personal, intimate or important than the decision to end one's life, especially when the reason for doing so is to avoid excessive and protracted pain. Accordingly, we believe the cases from *Pierce v. Society of Sisters* through *Roe* provide strong general support for our conclusion that a liberty interest in controlling the time and manner of one's death is protected by the Due Process Clause of the Fourteenth Amendment.

While the cases we have adverted to lend general support to our conclusion, we believe that two relatively recent decisions of the Court, *Casey* and *Cruzan*, are fully persuasive, and leave little doubt as to the proper result.

In *Casey*, the Court surveyed its prior decisions affording "constitutional protection to personal decisions relating to marriage, procreation, contraception, family relationships, child rearing, and education," and then said:

> These matters, involving the most intimate and personal choices a person may make in a lifetime, choices central to personal dignity and autonomy, are central to the liberty protected by the Fourteenth Amendment. At the heart of liberty is the right to define one's own concept of existence, of meaning, of the universe, and of the mystery of human life. Beliefs about these matters could not define the attributes of personhood were they formed under compulsion of the State.

The district judge [Rothstein] in this case found the Court's reasoning in *Casey* "highly instructive" and "almost prescriptive" for determining "what liberty interest may inhere in a terminally ill person's choice to commit suicide." We agree.

Like the decision of whether or not to have an abortion, the decision how and when to die is one of "the most intimate and personal choices a person may make in a lifetime," a choice "central to personal dignity and autonomy." A competent terminally ill adult, having lived nearly the full measure of his life, has a strong liberty interest in choosing a dignified and humane death rather than being reduced at the end of his existence to a childlike state of helplessness, diapered, sedated, incontinent. How a person dies not only determines the nature of the final period of his existence, but in many cases, the enduring memories held by those who love him.

Prohibiting a terminally ill patient from hastening his death may have an even more profound impact on that person's life than forcing a woman to carry a pregnancy to term.

The case of an AIDS patient treated by Dr. Peter Shalit, one of the physician-plaintiffs in this case, provides a compelling illustration. In his declaration, Dr. Shalit described his patient's death this way:

> One patient of mine, whom I will call Smith, a fictitious name, lingered in the hospital for weeks, his lower body so swollen from oozing Kaposi's lesions that he could not walk, his genitals so swollen that he required a catheter to drain his bladder, his fingers gangrenous from clotted arteries. Patient Smith's friends stopped visiting him because it gave them nightmares. Patient Smith's agonies could not be relieved by medication or by the excellent nursing care he received. Patient Smith begged for assistance in hastening his death. As his treating doctor, it was my professional opinion that patient Smith was mentally competent to make a choice with respect to shortening his period of suffering before inevitable death. I felt that I should accommodate his request. However, because of the statute, I was unable to assist him and he died after having been tortured for weeks by the end-phase of his disease.

For such patients, wracked by pain and deprived of all pleasure, a state-enforced prohibition on hastening their deaths condemns them to unrelieved misery or torture. Surely, a person's decision whether to endure or avoid such an existence constitutes one of the most, if not the most, "intimate and personal choices a person may make in a lifetime," a choice that is "central to personal dignity and autonomy." Surely such a decision implicates a most vital liberty interest.

In *Cruzan*, the Court considered whether or not there is a constitutionally-protected, due process liberty interest in terminating unwanted medical treatment. The Court said that an affirmative answer followed almost inevitably from its prior decisions holding that patients have a liberty interest in refusing to submit to specific medical procedures. Those cases include *Jacobsen v. Massachusetts*, in which the Court balanced an individual's liberty interest in declining an unwanted small pox vaccine against the State's interest in preventing disease; *Washington v. Harper*, in which the Court said: "The forcible injection of medication into a nonconsenting person's body represents a substantial interference with that person's liberty"; and *Parham v. J.R.*, in which it said: "[A] child, in common with adults, has a substantial liberty interest in not being confined unnecessarily for medical treatment." Writing for a majority that included Justices O'Connor and Scalia, Chief Justice Rehnquist said that those cases helped answer the first critical question at issue in *Cruzan*, stating: "The principle that a competent person has a constitutionally protected liberty interest in refusing unwanted medical treatment may be inferred from our prior decisions."

In her concurrence, Justice O'Connor explained that the majority opinion held (implicitly or otherwise) that a liberty interest in refusing medical treatment extends to all types of medical treatment from dialysis or artificial respirators to the provision of food and water by tube or other artificial means. As Justice O'Connor said: "I agree that a protected liberty interest in refusing unwanted medical treatment may be inferred from our prior decisions, and that the refusal of artificial delivery of food and water is encompassed in that liberty interest."

Justice O'Connor further concluded that under the majority's opinion, "[r]equiring a competent adult to endure such procedures against her will burdens the patient's liberty, dignity, and freedom to determine the course of her own treatment." In the majority opinion itself, Chief Justice Rehnquist made a similar assertion, writing:

> The choice between life and death is a deeply personal decision of obvious and overwhelming finality. We believe Missouri may legitimately seek to safeguard the personal element of this choice through the imposition of heightened evidentiary requirements. It cannot be disputed that the Due Process Clause protects an interest in life as well as an interest in refusing life-sustaining medical treatment.

These passages make it clear that *Cruzan* stands for the proposition that there is a due process liberty interest in rejecting unwanted medical treatment, including the provision of food and water by artificial means. Moreover, the Court majority clearly recognized that granting the request to remove the tubes through which Cruzan received artificial nutrition and hydration would lead inexorably to her death. Accordingly, we conclude that *Cruzan*, by recognizing a liberty interest that includes the refusal of artificial provision of life-sustaining food and water, necessarily recognizes a liberty interest in hastening one's own death.

Casey and *Cruzan* provide persuasive evidence that the Constitution encompasses a due process liberty interest in controlling the time and manner of one's death - that there is, in short, a constitutionally recognized "right to die." Our conclusion is strongly influenced by, but not limited to, the plight of mentally competent, terminally ill adults. We are influenced as well by the plight of others, such as those whose existence is reduced to a vegetative state or a permanent and irreversible state of unconsciousness.

Our conclusion that there is a liberty interest in determining the time and manner of one's death does not mean that there is a concomitant right to exercise that interest in all circumstances or to do so free from state regulation. To the contrary, we explicitly recognize that some prohibitory and regulatory state action is fully consistent with constitutional principles.

In short, finding a liberty interest constitutes a critical first step toward answering the question before us. The determination that must now be made is whether the state's attempt to curtail the exercise of that interest is constitutionally justified.

To determine whether a state action that impairs a liberty interest violates an individual's substantive due process rights we must identify the factors relevant to the case at hand, assess the state's interests and the individual's liberty interest in light of those factors, and then weigh and balance the competing interests. The relevant factors generally include: 1) the importance of the various state interests, both in general and in the factual context of the case; 2) the manner in which those interests are furthered by the state law or regulation; 3) the importance of the liberty interest, both in itself and in the context in which it is being exercised; 4) the extent to which that interest is burdened by the challenged state action; and, 5) the consequences of upholding or overturning the statute or regulation.

We analyze the factors in turn, and begin by considering the first: the importance of the state's interests. We identify six related state interests involved in the controversy before us: 1) the state's general interest in preserving life; 2) the state's more specific interest in preventing suicide; 3) the state's interest in avoiding the involvement of third parties and in precluding the use of arbitrary, unfair, or undue influence;

4) the state's interest in protecting family members and loved ones; 5) the state's interest in protecting the integrity of the medical profession; and, 6) the state's interest in avoiding adverse consequences that might ensue if the statutory provision at issue is declared unconstitutional.

The state may assert an unqualified interest in preserving life in general. As the Court said in *Cruzan*, "we think a State may properly decline to make judgments about the 'quality' of life that a particular individual may enjoy, and simply assert an unqualified interest in the preservation of human life . . ." . Thus, the state may assert its interest in preserving life in all cases, including those of terminally ill, competent adults who wish to hasten their deaths.

Although the state's interest in preserving life may be unqualified, and may be asserted regardless of the quality of the life or lives at issue, that interest is not always controlling. Nor is it of the same strength in each case. To the contrary, its strength is dependent on relevant circumstances, including the medical condition and the wishes of the person whose life is at stake.

Most tellingly, the state of Washington has already decided that its interest in preserving life should ordinarily give way - at least in the case of competent, terminally ill adults who are dependent on medical treatment - to the wishes of the patients. In its Natural Death Act, Washington permits adults to have "life-sustaining treatment withheld or withdrawn in instances of a terminal condition or permanent unconsciousness." In adopting the statute, the Washington legislature necessarily determined that the state's interest in preserving life is not so weighty that it ought to thwart the informed desire of a terminally ill, competent adult to refuse medical treatment.

Not only does Washington law acknowledge that terminally ill and permanently unconscious adults have a right to refuse life-sustaining treatment, the statute includes specific legislative findings that appear to recognize that a due process liberty interest underlies that right. The statute states:

> The legislature finds that adult persons have the fundamental right to control the decisions relating to the rendering of their own medical care, including the decision to have life-sustaining procedures withheld or withdrawn in instances of terminal condition.

> The legislature further finds that modern medical technology has made possible the artificial prolongation of human life beyond natural limits.

> The legislature further finds that, in the interest of protecting individual autonomy, such prolongation of life for persons with a terminal condition may cause loss of patient dignity, and unnecessary pain and suffering, while providing nothing medically necessary or beneficial to the patient.

The Washington statute permits competent adults to reject life-sustaining medical treatment in advance by means of living wills and durable powers of attorney. Even in cases in which the Washington Natural Death Act does not authorize surrogate decision-making, the Washington Supreme Court has found that legal guardians may sometimes have life-sustaining treatment discontinued.

There is nothing unusual about Washington's recognition that the state's interest in preserving life is not always of the same force and that in some cases at least other considerations may outweigh the state's. More than 40 other states have adopted living will statutes that permit competent adults to declare by advance directive that they do not wish to be kept alive by medical treatment in the latter stages of a terminal illness. Like Washington, many states also permit competent adults to determine in advance that they do not wish any medical treatment should they become permanently and irreversibly unconscious. Also, like Washington, many states allow patients to delegate decision-making power to a surrogate through a durable power of attorney, health care proxy, or similar device, or permit courts to appoint surrogate decision-makers. Finally, Congress favors permitting adult patients to refuse life-sustaining treatment by advance directive and requires hospitals receiving federal financial support to notify adult patients of their rights to execute such instruments upon admission.

As the laws in state after state demonstrate, even though the protection of life is one of the state's most important functions, the state's interest is dramatically diminished if the person it seeks to protect is terminally ill or permanently comatose and has expressed a wish that he be permitted to die without further medical treatment (or if a duly appointed representative has done so on his behalf). When patients are no longer able to pursue liberty or happiness and do not wish to pursue life, the state's interest in forcing them to remain alive is clearly less compelling. Thus, while the state may still seek to prolong the lives of terminally ill or comatose patients or, more likely, to enact regulations that will safeguard the manner in which decisions to hasten death are made, the strength of the state's interest is substantially reduced in such circumstances.

While the state's general commitment to the preservation of life clearly encompasses the prevention of suicide, the state has an even more particular interest in deterring the taking of one's own life. The fact that neither Washington nor any other state currently bans suicide, or attempted suicide, does not mean that the state does not have a valid and important interest in preventing or discouraging that act.

During the course of this litigation, the state has relied on its interest in the prevention of suicide as its primary justification for its statute. The state points to statistics concerning the rate of suicide among various age groups, particularly the young. As the state notes, in 1991, suicide was the second leading cause of death after accidents for the age groups 15-19, 20-24, and 25-34 and one of the top five causes of death for age groups 35-44 and 45-54. These figures are indeed distressing.

Although suicide by teenagers and young adults is especially tragic, the state has a clear interest in preventing anyone, no matter what age, from taking his own life in a fit of desperation, depression, or loneliness or as a result of any other problem, physical or psychological, which can be significantly ameliorated. Studies show that many suicides are committed by people who are suffering from treatable mental disorders. Most if not all states provide for the involuntary commitment of such persons if they are likely to physically harm themselves. For similar reasons, at least a dozen states allow the use of nondeadly force to prevent suicide attempts.

While the state has a legitimate interest in preventing suicides in general, that interest, like the state's interest in preserving life, is substantially diminished in the case of terminally ill, competent adults who wish to die. One of the heartaches of suicide is the senseless loss of a life ended prematurely. In the case of a terminally ill adult who ends his life in the final stages of an incurable and painful degenerative disease, in order to avoid debilitating pain and a humiliating death, the decision to commit suicide is not senseless, and death does not come too early. Unlike "the depressed twenty-one year old, the romantically devastated twenty-eight year old, the alcoholic forty-year old," or many others who may be inclined to commit suicide, a terminally ill competent adult cannot be cured. While some people who contemplate suicide can be restored to a state of physical and mental well-being, terminally ill adults who wish to die can only be maintained in a debilitated and deteriorating state, unable to enjoy the presence of family or friends. Not only is the state's interest in preventing such individuals from hastening their deaths of comparatively little weight, but its insistence on frustrating their wishes seems cruel indeed. As Kent said in *King Lear*, when signs of life were seen in the dying monarch:

> Vex not his ghost: O! let him pass; he hate him
> That would upon the rack of this tough world
> Stretch him out longer.

The state has explicitly recognized that its interests are frequently insufficient to override the wishes of competent, terminally ill adult patients who desire to bring their lives to an end with the assistance of a physician. Step by step, the state has acknowledged that terminally ill persons are entitled in a whole variety of circumstances to hasten their deaths, and that in such cases their physicians may assist in the process. Until relatively recently, while physicians routinely helped patients to hasten their deaths, they did so discretely because almost all such assistance was illegal. However, beginning about twenty years ago a series of dramatic changes took place. Each provoked the type of division and debate that surrounds the issue before us today. Each time the state's interests were ultimately subordinated to the liberty interests of the individual, in part as a result of legal actions and in part as a result of a growing recognition by the medical community and society at large that a more enlightened approach was essential.

The first major breakthrough occurred when the terminally ill were permitted to reject medical treatment. The line was drawn initially at extraordinary medical treatment because the distinction between ordinary and extraordinary treatment appeared to some to offer the courts an objective, scientific standard that would enable them to recognize the right to refuse certain medical treatment without also recognizing a right to suicide or euthanasia. That distinction, however, quickly proved unworkable, and after a while, terminally ill patients were allowed to reject *both* extraordinary and ordinary treatment. For a while, *rejection* of treatment, often through "do not resuscitate" orders, was permitted, but *termination* was not. This dividing line, which rested on the illusory distinction between commission and omission (or active and passive), also appeared for a short time to offer a natural point of repose for doctors, patients and the law. However, it, too, quickly proved untenable, and ultimately patients were allowed both to *refuse* and to *terminate* medical treatment, ordinary as well as extraordinary. Today, many states also allow the terminally ill to order their physicians to discontinue not just traditional medical treatment but the artificial provision of life-sustaining food and water, thus permitting the patients to die by self-starvation. Equally important, today, doctors are generally permitted to administer death-inducing medication, as long as they can point to a concomitant pain-relieving purpose.

In light of these drastic changes regarding acceptable medical practices, opponents of physician-assisted suicide must now explain precisely what it is about the physician's conduct in assisted suicide cases that distinguishes it from the conduct that the state has explicitly authorized. The state responds by urging that physician-assisted suicide is different in kind, not degree, from the type of physician-life-ending conduct that is now authorized, for three separate reasons. It argues that "assisted suicide": 1) requires doctors to play an active role; 2) causes deaths that would not result from the patient's underlying disease; and 3) requires doctors to provide the causal agent of patients' deaths.

The distinctions suggested by the state do not individually or collectively serve to distinguish the medical practices society currently accepts. The first distinction - the line between commission and omission - is a distinction without a difference now that patients are permitted not only to decline all medical treatment, but to instruct their doctors to *terminate* whatever treatment, artificial or otherwise, they are receiving. In disconnecting a respirator, or authorizing its disconnection, a doctor is unquestionably *committing* an act; he is taking an *active* role in bringing about the patient's death. In fact, there can be no doubt that in such instances the doctor intends that, as the result of his action, the patient will die an earlier death than he otherwise would.

Similarly, drawing a distinction on the basis of whether the patient's death results from an underlying disease no longer has any legitimacy. While the distinction may once have seemed tenable, at least from a metaphysical standpoint, it was not based on a valid or practical legal foundation and was therefore quickly abandoned. When Nancy Cruzan's feeding and hydration tube was removed, she did not die of an underlying disease. Rather, she was allowed to starve to death. In fact, Ms. Cruzan was not even terminally ill at the time, but had a life expectancy of 30 years. Similarly, when a doctor provides a conscious patient with medication to ease his discomfort while he starves himself to death - a practice that is not only legal but has been urged as an alternative to assisted suicide - the patient does not die of any underlying ailment. To the contrary, the doctor is helping the patient end his life by providing medication that makes it possible for the patient to achieve suicide by starvation.

Nor is the state's third and final distinction valid. Contrary to the state's assertion, given current medical practices and current medical ethics, it is not possible to distinguish prohibited from permissible medical conduct on the basis of whether the medication provided by the doctor will cause the patient's death. As part of the tradition of administering comfort care, doctors have been supplying the causal agent of patients' deaths for decades. Physicians routinely and openly provide medication to terminally ill patients with the knowledge that it will have a "double effect" - reduce the patient's pain and hasten his death. Such medical treatment is accepted by the medical profession as meeting its highest ethical standards. It commonly takes the form of putting a patient on an intravenous morphine drip, with full knowledge that, while such treatment will alleviate his pain, it will also indubitably hasten his death. There can be no doubt, therefore, that the actual cause of the patient's death is the drug administered by the physician or by a person acting under his supervision or direction. Thus, the causation argument is simply "another bridge crossed" in the journey to vindicate the liberty interests of the terminally ill, and the state's third distinction has no more force than the other two.

We acknowledge that in some respects a recognition of the legitimacy of physician-assisted suicide would constitute an additional step beyond what the courts have previously approved. We also acknowledge that judicial acceptance of physician-assisted suicide would cause many sincere persons with strong moral or religious convictions great distress. Nevertheless, we do not believe that the state's interest in preventing that additional step is significantly greater than its interest in preventing the other forms of life-ending medical conduct that doctors now engage in regularly. More specifically, we see little, if any, difference for constitutional or ethical purposes between providing medication with a double effect and providing medication with a single effect, as long as one of the known effects in each case is to hasten the end of the patient's life. Similarly, we see no ethical or constitutionally cognizable difference between a doctor's pulling the plug on a respirator and his prescribing drugs which will permit a terminally ill patient to end his own life. In fact, some might argue that pulling the plug is a more culpable and aggressive act on the doctor's part and provides more reason for criminal prosecution. To us, what matters most is that the death of the patient is the intended result as surely in one case as in the other. In sum, we find the state's interests in preventing suicide do not make its interests substantially stronger here than in cases involving other forms of death-hastening medical intervention. To the extent that a difference exists, we conclude that it is one of degree and not of kind.

Moreover, we are doubtful that deaths resulting from terminally ill patients taking medication prescribed by their doctors should be classified as "suicide." Certainly, we see little basis for such a classification when deaths that result from patients' decisions to terminate life support systems or to refuse life-sustaining food and water, for example, are not. We believe that there is a strong argument that a decision by a terminally ill patient to hasten by medical means a death that is already in process, should not be classified as suicide. Thus, notwithstanding the generally accepted use of the term "physician-assisted suicide," we have serious doubt that the state's interest in preventing suicide is even implicated in this case.

In addition to the state's purported interest in preventing suicide, it has an additional interest in preventing deaths that occur as a result of errors in medical or legal judgment. We acknowledge that it is sometimes impossible to predict with certainty the duration of a terminally ill patient's remaining existence, just as it is sometimes impossible to say for certain whether a borderline individual is or is not mentally competent. However, we believe that sufficient safeguards can and will be developed by the state and medical profession to ensure that the possibility of error will ordinarily be remote. Finally, although life and death decisions are of the gravest order, should an error actually occur it is likely to benefit the individual by permitting a victim of unmanageable pain and suffering to end his life peacefully and with dignity at the time he deems most desirable.

A state may properly assert an interest in prohibiting even altruistic assistance to a person contemplating suicide on the grounds that allowing others to help may increase the incidence of suicide, undercut society's commitment to the sanctity of life, and, adversely affect the person providing the assistance. In addition, joint action is generally considered more serious than action by a single person. While we recognize that these concerns are legitimate, the most important - the first two - diminish in importance to the same extent that the state's interest in preventing the act itself diminishes. All are at their minimums when the assistance is provided by or under the supervision or direction of a doctor and the recipient is a terminally ill patient.

In upholding Washington's statute, the majority of the three-judge panel relied heavily on the state's interest in preventing the exercise of undue, arbitrary or unfair influences over the individual's decision to end his life. We agree that this is an important interest, but for entirely different reasons than the majority suggests. One of the majority's prime arguments is that the statute is necessary to protect "the poor and minorities from exploitation," - in other words, to protect the disadvantaged from becoming the victims of assisted suicide. This rationale simply recycles one of the more disingenuous and fallacious arguments raised in opposition to the legalization of abortion. It is equally meretricious here. In fact, as with abortion, there is far more reason to raise the opposite concern: the concern that the poor and the minorities, who have historically received the least adequate health care, will not be afforded a fair opportunity to obtain the medical assistance to which they are entitled - the assistance that would allow them to end their lives with a measure of dignity. The argument that disadvantaged persons will receive *more* medical services than the remainder of the population in one, and only one, area - assisted suicide - is ludicrous on its face. So, too, is the argument that the poor and the minorities will rush to volunteer for physician-assisted suicide because of their inability to secure adequate medical treatment.

Our analysis is similar regarding the argument relating to the handicapped. Again, the opponents of physician-assisted suicide urge a variation of the discredited anti-abortion argument. Despite the dire predictions, the disabled were not pressured into seeking abortions. Nor is it likely that the disabled will be pressured into committing physician-assisted suicide. Organizations representing the physically impaired are sufficiently active politically and sufficiently vigilant that they would soon put a halt to any effort to employ assisted suicide in a manner that affected their clients unfairly. There are other more subtle concerns, however, advanced by some representatives of the physically impaired, including the fear that certain physical disabilities will erroneously be deemed to make life "valueless." While we recognize the legitimacy of these concerns, we also recognize that seriously impaired individuals will, along with non-impaired individuals, be the beneficiaries of the liberty interest asserted here - and that if they are not afforded the option to control their own fate, they like many others will be compelled, against their will, to endure unusual and protracted suffering. The resolution that would be best for all, of course, would be to ensure that the practice of assisted suicide is conducted fairly and well, and that adequate safeguards sufficient to avoid the feared abuses are adopted and enforced.

There is a far more serious concern regarding third parties that we must consider - one not even mentioned by the majority in the panel opinion. That concern is the fear that infirm, elderly persons will come under undue pressure to end their lives from callous, financially burdened, or self-interested relatives, or others who have influence over them. The risk of undue influence is real - and it exists today. Persons with a stake in the outcome may now pressure the terminally ill to reject or decline life-saving treatment or take other steps likely to hasten their demise. Surrogates may make unfeeling life and death decisions for their incompetent relatives. This concern deserves serious consideration, as it did when the decision was made some time ago to permit the termination of life-support systems and the withdrawal or withholding of other forms of medical treatment, and when it was decided to recognize living wills, durable powers of attorney, and the right of courts to appoint substitute decision-makers. While we do not minimize the concern, the temptation to exert undue pressure is ordinarily tempered to a substantial degree in the case of the terminally ill by the knowledge that the person will die shortly in any event. Given the possibility of undue influence that already exists, the recognition of the right to physician-assisted suicide would not increase that risk unduly. In fact, the direct involvement of an impartial and professional third party in the decision-making process would more likely provide an important safeguard against such abuse.

We also realize that terminally ill patients may well feel pressured to hasten their deaths, not because of improper conduct by their loved ones, but rather for an opposite reason - out of concern for the economic welfare of their loved ones. Faced with the prospect of astronomical medical bills, terminally ill patients might decide that it is better for them to die before their health care expenses consume the life savings they planned to leave for their families, or, worse yet, burden their families with debts they may never be able to satisfy. While state regulations can help ensure that patients do not make rash, uninformed, or ill considered decisions, we are reluctant to say that, in a society in which the costs of protracted health care can be so exorbitant, it is improper for competent, terminally ill adults to take the economic welfare of their families and loved ones into consideration.

. . . . As members of the judicial branch, however, we are compelled to stand aside from that battle. On the other hand, we are certainly not obligated to pile injury upon injury by holding that all of our citizens may be subjected to the prospect of needless pain, suffering, and degradation at the end of their lives, either because of our concern over Congress' failure to provide government-insured health care or alternatively in order to satisfy the moral or religious precepts of a portion of the population.

We are also aware of the concern that doctors become hardened to the inevitability of death and to the plight of terminally ill patients, and that they will treat requests to die in a routine and impersonal manner, rather than affording the careful, thorough, individualized attention that each request deserves. The day of the family doctor who made house calls and knew the frailties and strengths of each family member is long gone. So, too, in the main, is the intense personal interest that doctors used to take in their patients' welfare and activities. Doctors like the rest of society face constantly increasing pressures, and may not always have the patience to deal with the elderly, some of whom can be both difficult and troublesome. Nevertheless, there are many doctors who specialize in geriatric care and there are many more who are not specialists but who treat elderly patients with great compassion and sensitivity. We believe that most, if not all, doctors would not assist a terminally ill patient to hasten his death as long as there were any reasonable chance of alleviating the patient's suffering or enabling him to live under tolerable conditions. We also believe that physicians would not assist a patient to end his life if there were any significant doubt about the patient's true wishes. To do so would be contrary to the physicians' fundamental training, their conservative nature, and the ethics of their profession. In any case, since doctors are highly-regulated professionals, it should not be difficult for the state or the profession itself to establish rules and procedures that will ensure that the occasional negligent or careless recommendation by a licensed physician will not result in an uninformed or erroneous decision by the patient or his family.

Having said all this, we do not dismiss the legitimate concerns that exist regarding undue influence. While steps can be taken to minimize the danger substantially, the concerns cannot be wholly eliminated. Accordingly, they are of more than minimal weight and, in balancing the competing interests, we treat them seriously.

The state clearly has a legitimate interest in safeguarding the interests of innocent third parties such as minor children and other family members dependent on persons who wish to commit suicide. That state interest, however, is of almost negligible weight when the patient is terminally ill and his death is imminent and inevitable. The state cannot help a minor child or any other innocent third party by forcing a terminally ill patient to die a more protracted and painful death. In fact, witnessing a loved one suffer a slow and agonizing death as a result of state compulsion is more likely to harm than further the interests of innocent third parties.

The state has a legitimate interest in assuring the integrity of the medical profession, an interest that includes prohibiting physicians from engaging in conduct that is at odds with their role as healers. We do not believe that the integrity of the medical profession would be threatened in any way by the vindication of the liberty interest at issue here. Rather, it is the existence of a statute that criminalizes the provision of medical assistance to patients in need that could create conflicts with the doctors' professional obligations and make covert criminals out of honorable, dedicated, and compassionate individuals.

The assertion that the legalization of physician-assisted suicide will erode the commitment of doctors to help their patients rests both on an ignorance of what numbers of doctors have been doing for a considerable time and on a misunderstanding of the proper function of a physician. As we have previously noted, doctors have been discretely helping terminally ill patients hasten their deaths for decades and probably centuries, while acknowledging privately that there was no other medical purpose to their actions. They have done so with the tacit approval of a substantial percentage of both the public and the medical profession, and without in any way diluting their commitment to their patients.

In addition, as we also noted earlier, doctors may now openly take actions that will result in the deaths of their patients. They may terminate life-support systems, withdraw life-sustaining gastronomy tubes, otherwise terminate or withhold all other forms of medical treatment, and, may even administer lethal doses of drugs with full knowledge of their "double effect." Given the similarity between what doctors are now permitted to do and what the plaintiffs assert they should be permitted to do, we see no risk at all to the integrity of the profession. This is a conclusion that is shared by a growing number of doctors who openly support physician-assisted suicide and proclaim it to be fully compatible with the physicians' calling and with their commitment and obligation to help the sick. Many more doctors support physician-assisted suicide but without openly advocating a change in the legal treatment of the practice. A recent study of Oregon physicians found that 60% of those who responded believed that physician-assisted suicide should be legal. A recent study of attitudes among physicians in Michigan, where the state legislature adopted a law banning assisted-suicide as a result of Dr. Jack Kevorkian's activities, found that only 17.2% of the physicians who responded favored a law prohibiting assisted-suicide. Almost all the rest supported one of three options: legalizing physician-assisted suicide (38.9%); permitting the medical profession to regulate the practice (16.1%); or leaving decisions about physician-assisted suicide to the doctor-patient relationship (16.6%). Thus over 70% of the Michigan doctors answering the poll appear to believe that professional ethics do not preclude doctors from engaging in acts that today are classified as "assisted suicide." Even among those doctors who oppose assisted suicide medical ethics do not lie at the heart of the objections. The "most important personal characteristic" separating those doctors from their colleagues is a strong religious identification.

Whether or not a patient can be cured, the doctor has an obligation to attempt to alleviate his pain and suffering. If it is impossible to cure the patient or retard the advance of his disease, then the doctor's primary duty is to make the patient as comfortable as possible. When performing that task, the doctor is performing a proper medical function, even though he knows that his patient's death is a necessary and inevitable consequence of his actions.

. . . [T]he American Medical Association filed an amicus [friend of the court] brief urging that we uphold the practice of administering medicine with a dual effect. At the same time, it takes the position that physician-assisted suicide should not be legalized, at least as of this time. Twenty years ago, the AMA contended that performing abortions violated the Hippocratic Oath; today, it claims that assisting terminally ill patients to hasten their death does likewise. Clearly, the Hippocratic Oath can have no greater import in deciding the constitutionality of physician assisted-suicide than it did in determining whether women had a constitutional right to have an abortion. In *Roe*, the Court cited a scholar's conclusion that the Hippocratic Oath "originated in a group representing only a small segment of Greek opinion and that it certainly was not accepted by all ancient physicians." The Court stressed the Oath's "rigidity" and was not deterred by its prohibitory language regarding abortion. As *Roe* shows, a literalist reading of the Hippocratic Oath does not represent the best or final word on medical or legal controversies today. Were we to adhere to the rigid language of the oath, not only would doctors be barred from performing abortions or helping terminally ill patients hasten their deaths, but according to a once-accepted interpretation, they would also be prohibited from performing any type of surgery at all, a position that would now be recognized as preposterous by even the most tradition-bound AMA members. More important, regardless of the AMA or its position, experience shows that most doctors can readily adapt to a changing legal climate. Once the Court held that a woman has a constitutional right to have an abortion, doctors began performing abortions routinely and the ethical integrity of the medical profession remained undiminished. Similarly, following the recognition of a constitutional right to assisted suicide, we believe that doctors would engage in the permitted practice when appropriate, and that the integrity of the medical profession would survive without blemish.

Recognizing the right to "assisted-suicide" would not require doctors to do anything contrary to their individual principles. A physician whose moral or religious beliefs would prevent him from assisting a patient to hasten his death would be free to follow the dictates of his conscience. Those doctors who believe that terminally ill, competent, adult patients should be permitted to choose the time and manner of their death would be able to help them do so. We believe that extending a choice to doctors as well as to patients would help protect the integrity of the medical profession without compromising the rights or principles of individual doctors and without sacrificing the welfare of their patients.

We now consider the state's final concern. Those opposed to permitting physician-assisted suicide often point to a concern that could be subsumed under the state's general interest in preserving life, but which for clarity's sake we treat separately. The argument is a purely pragmatic one that causes many people deep concern: permitting physician-assisted suicide would "open Pandora's Box."

Once we recognize a liberty interest in hastening one's death, the argument goes, that interest will sweep away all restrictions in its wake. It will only be a matter of time, the argument continues, before courts will sanction putting people to death, not because they are desperately ill and want to die, but because they are deemed to pose an unjustifiable burden on society. Known as a slippery slope argument or what one commentator has called the "thin edge of the wedge" argument, the opponents of assisted-suicide conjure up a parade of horribles and insist that the only way to halt the downward spiral is to stop it before it starts.

This same nihilistic argument can be offered against any constitutionally-protected right or interest. Both before and after women were found to have a right to have an abortion, critics contended that legalizing that medical procedure would lead to its widespread use as a substitute for other forms of birth control or as a means of racial genocide. Inflammatory contentions regarding ways in which the recognition of the right would lead to the ruination of the country did not, however, deter the Supreme Court from first recognizing and then two decades later reaffirming a constitutionally-protected liberty interest in terminating an unwanted pregnancy. In fact, the Court has *never* refused to recognize a substantive due process liberty right or interest merely because there were difficulties in determining when and how to limit its exercise or because others might someday attempt to use it improperly.

Recognition of any right creates the possibility of abuse. The slippery slope fears of *Roe's* opponents have, of course, not materialized. The legalization of abortion has not undermined our commitment to life generally; nor, as some predicted, has it led to widespread infanticide. Similarly, there is no reason to believe that legalizing assisted suicide will lead to the horrific consequences its opponents suggest.

The slippery slope argument also comes in a second and closely related form. This version of the argument states that a due process interest in hastening one's death, even if the exercise of that interest is initially limited to the terminally ill, will prove infinitely expansive because it will be impossible to define the term "terminally ill." (After all, all of us are terminal in some sense of the word, are we not?) The argument rests on two false premises. First it presupposes a need for greater precision than is required in constitutional law. Second, it assumes that the terms "terminal illness" or "terminal condition" cannot be defined, even though those terms have in fact been defined repeatedly. They have, for example, been defined in a model statute, The Uniform Rights of the Terminally Ill Act, and in more than 40 state natural death statutes, including Washington's. The model statute and some of the state statutes have defined the term without reference to a fixed time period; others have taken the opposite approach, defining terminal to mean that death is likely to ensue within six months. As we have noted earlier, the Washington Act, like some others, includes persons who are permanently unconscious, that is in an irreversible coma or a persistent vegetative state. While defining the term "terminally ill" is not free from difficulty, the experience of the states has proved that the class of the terminally ill is neither indefinable nor undefined. Indeed, all of the persons described in the various statutes would appear to fall within an appropriate definition of the term. In any event, it is apparent that purported definitional difficulties that have repeatedly been surmounted provide no legitimate reason for refusing to recognize a liberty interest in hastening one's death.

We do not dispute the . . . contention that the prescription of lethal medication by physicians for use by terminally ill patients who wish to die does not constitute a clear point of demarcation between permissible and impermissible medical conduct. We agree that it may be difficult to make a principled distinction between physician-assisted suicide and the provision to terminally ill patients of other forms of life-ending medical assistance, such as the administration of drugs by a physician. We recognize that in some instances, the patient may be unable to self-administer the drugs and that administration by the physician, or a person acting under his direction or control, may be the only way the patient may be able to receive them. The question whether that type of physician conduct may be constitutionally prohibited must be answered directly in future cases, and not in this one. We would be less than candid, however, if we did not acknowledge that for present purposes we view the critical line in right-to-die cases as the one between the voluntary and involuntary termination of an individual's life. In the first case - volitional death - the physician is aiding or assisting a patient who wishes to exercise a liberty interest, and in the other - involuntary death - another person acting on his own behalf, or, in some instances society's, is determining that an individual's life should no longer continue. We consider it less important who administers the medication than who determines whether the terminally ill person's life shall end. In any event, here we decide only the issue before us - the constitutionality of prohibiting doctors from prescribing medication for use by terminally ill patients who wish to hasten their death.

In applying the balancing test, we must take into account not only the strength of the state's interests but also the means by which the state has chosen to further those interests.

Washington's statute prohibiting assisted suicide has a drastic impact on the terminally ill. By prohibiting physician assistance, it bars what for many terminally ill patients is the only palatable, and only practical, way to end their lives. Physically frail, confined to wheelchairs or beds, many terminally ill patients do not have the means or ability to kill themselves in the multitude of ways that healthy individuals can. Often, for example, they cannot even secure the medication or devices they would need to carry out their wishes.

Some terminally ill patients stockpile prescription medicine, which they can use to end their lives when they decide the time is right. The successful use of the stockpile technique generally depends, however, on the assistance of a physician, whether tacit or unknowing (although it is *possible* to end one's life with over-the-counter medication). Even if the terminally ill patients are able to accumulate sufficient drugs, given the pain killers and other medication they are taking, most of them would lack the knowledge to determine what dose of any given drug or drugs they must take, or in what combination. Miscalculation can be tragic. It can lead to an even more painful and lingering death. Alternatively, if the medication reduces respiration enough to restrict the flow of oxygen to the brain but not enough to cause death, it can result in the patient's falling into a comatose or vegetative state.

Thus for many terminally ill patients, the Washington statute is effectively a prohibition. While technically it only prohibits one means of exercising a liberty interest, practically it prohibits the exercise of that interest as effectively as prohibiting doctors from performing abortions prevented women from having abortions in the days before *Roe*.

State laws or regulations governing physician-assisted suicide are both necessary and desirable to ensure against errors and abuse, and to protect legitimate state interests. Any of several model statutes might serve as an example of how these legitimate and important concerns can be addressed effectively.

By adopting appropriate, reasonable, and properly drawn safeguards Washington could ensure that people who choose to have their doctors prescribe lethal doses of medication are truly competent and meet all of the requisite standards. Without endorsing the constitutionality of any particular procedural safeguards, we note that the state might, for example, require: witnesses to ensure voluntariness; reasonable, though short, waiting periods to prevent rash decisions; second medical opinions to confirm a patient's terminal status and also to confirm that the patient has been receiving proper treatment, including adequate comfort care; psychological examinations to ensure that the patient is not suffering from momentary or treatable depression; reporting procedures that will aid in the avoidance of abuse. Alternatively, such safeguards could be adopted by interested medical associations and other organizations involved in the provision of health care, so long as they meet the state's needs and concerns.

While there is always room for error in any human endeavor, we believe that sufficient protections can and will be developed by the various states, with the assistance of the medical profession and health care industry, to ensure that the possibility of error will be remote. We do not expect that, in this nation, the development of appropriate statutes and regulations will be taken lightly by any of the interested parties, or that those charged with their enforcement will fail to perform their duties properly.

In treating a prohibition differently from a regulation, we are following the approach that the Court took in the only right-to-die case to come before it. In *Cruzan*, the Court recognized that the states had a legitimate role to play in regulating the process of refusing or terminating life-sustaining medical treatment even if they could not prohibit the making of decisions that met applicable state standards. The Court explicitly recognized that states did not have to refrain from acting, but rather could adopt appropriate regulations to further their legitimate interests. Missouri's requirement for clear and convincing evidence of a patient's wishes was a regulation designed to reduce the risk of erroneous decisions. The Court upheld that regulation, a requirement that, of course, had far less impact on the exercise of the due process liberty interest than the de facto [actual] prohibition at issue here.

To those who argue that courts should refrain from declaring that the terminally ill have a constitutional right to physician-assisted suicide and that we should leave such matters to the individual states, we reply that where important liberty interests are at stake it is not the proper role of the state to adopt statutes totally prohibiting their exercise. Rather, the state should enact regulatory measures that ensure that the exercise of those interests is properly circumscribed and that all necessary safeguards have been provided. In the case of abortions and in the case of the withdrawal of life-sustaining medical treatment, the Court permitted states to enact appropriate regulations that would further its legitimate interests. In this case, like the others, the guiding principle is found in the words of Justice O'Connor [in her concurring opinion in *Cruzan*]. "[T]he more challenging task of crafting appropriate procedures for safeguarding . . . [terminally ill patients'] liberty interests is entrusted to the 'laboratory' of the states in the first instance."

Earlier in the opinion we described the liberty interest at issue here and explained its importance. We also explained that the strength of that interest is dependent on a number of factors, especially the individual's physical condition. We noted that an individual's liberty interest in hastening his death is at its low point when that person is young and healthy, because forcing a robust individual to continue living does not, at least absent extraordinary circumstances, subject him to "pain . . . [and] suffering that is too intimate and personal for the State to insist on . . . ." As we also made clear, when a mentally competent adult is terminally ill, and wishes, free of any coercion, to hasten his death because his remaining days are an unmitigated torture, that person's liberty interest is at its height. For such a person, being forced to live is indeed being subjected to "pain . . . [and] suffering that is too intimate and personal for the State to insist on . . . ."

We have also previously discussed at some length the nature and extent of the burden that the Washington statute imposes on the liberty interest. Here, we need only mention some of the specific evidence introduced by the plaintiffs and refer to some of our earlier analysis. The plaintiffs offered considerable specific testimony involving individual patients that strongly supports their claims that the Washington statute frequently presents an insuperable obstacle to terminally ill persons who wish to hasten their deaths by peaceful means. The testimony produced by the plaintiffs shows that many terminally ill patients who wish to die with dignity are forced to resort to gruesome alternatives because of the unavailability of physician assistance. One such patient, a 34-year-old man dying from AIDS and lymphoma, asked his physician for drugs to hasten his inevitable death after enduring four excruciatingly painful months because he did not wish to die in a hospital in a drug-induced stupor. His doctor, Dr. Harold Glucksberg, one of the physician plaintiffs in this case, refused because he feared prosecution under [Washington's statute]. Denied medical assistance, the patient ended his life by jumping from the West Seattle bridge and plummeting to his death. Fortunately, he did not survive the plunge and require permanent hospitalization in an even more exacerbated state of pain.

Deprived of physician assistance, another terminally ill patient took his own life by withholding his insulin and letting himself die of insulin shock. Like many terminally ill patients, one individual killed himself in a secretive and lonely fashion, in order to spare his family from possible criminal charges; as a result he was deprived of a chance to die in a dignified manner with his loved ones at his side. The man's daughter described her father's death this way:

> When he realized that my family was going to be away for a day, he wrote us a beautiful letter, went down to his basement, and shot himself with his 12 gauge shot gun. He was 84. . . . My son-in-law then had the unfortunate and unpleasant task of cleaning my father's splattered brains off the basement walls.

The plaintiffs also produced testimony showing that some terminally ill patients who try to kill themselves are unsuccessful, maiming instead of killing themselves, or that they succeed only after subjecting themselves to needless, excruciating pain. One such terminally ill patient, a mentally competent woman in her 80s suffering from metastatic breast cancer, sought medication to hasten her death from her primary care physician, Dr. Abigail Halperin, one of the physician plaintiffs in this case. Although Dr. Halperin believed, in her professional judgment, that she should accommodate her patient's wishes, she did not do so because she feared prosecution under [Washington's] statute. The patient acted on her own to hasten her death by placing a plastic bag over her head, securing it so no more air could enter. She suffocated to death, an end that was certainly more painful and inhumane than the death she would have experienced had she been given the prescriptions she sought.

Next, the plaintiffs produced testimony showing that many terminally ill patients are physically or psychologically unable to take their lives by the violent means that are almost always their only alternatives in the absence of assistance from a physician. One man declared that his terminally ill wife "wanted to die but we did not know how to do it. We could not ask her doctors. . . . She feared over-the-counter pills, hearing of all the cases where the person woke up a vegetable. Carbon monoxide was out since she wanted the dignity of dying in her own bed, surrounded by the things she loved." Another woman told how her father, "to whom dignity was very important, lay dying, diapered, moaning in pain, begging to die."

Following the approach of the Court in *Casey*, we note that there is also an extensive body of legal, medical, and sociological literature, lending support to the conclusion that a prohibition on physician assistance imposes an onerous burden on terminally ill, competent adults who wish to hasten their deaths. That conclusion is further buttressed by extensive anecdotal evidence compiled in newspapers and magazines. Although the statute at issue does not totally prohibit the exercise of the liberty interest by all who possess it, it does effectively prohibit its exercise by almost all of the terminally ill. In fact, as applied, the ban on the liberty interest is close to complete; for, there are few terminally ill persons who do not obtain illicit help from someone in the course of their efforts to hasten their deaths.

There is an additional burden on loved ones and family members that is often overlooked. Some terminally ill persons enlist their children, parents, or others who care for them deeply, in an agonizing, brutal and damaging endeavor, criminalized by the state, to end their pain and suffering. The loving and dedicated persons who agree to help - even if they are fortunate enough to avoid prosecution, and almost all are - will likely suffer pain and guilt for the rest of their lives. Those who decline to assist may always wonder whether they should have tried to save their parent or mate from enduring, unnecessary and protracted agony. This burden would be substantially alleviated if doctors were authorized to assist terminally ill persons to end their lives and to supervise and direct others in the implementation of that process.

In various earlier sections of this opinion, we have discussed most of the consequences of upholding or overturning the Washington statutory provision at issue, because in this case those consequences are best considered as part of the discussion of the specific factors or interests. The one remaining consequence of significance is easy to identify: Whatever the outcome here, a host of painful and agonizing issues involving the right to die will continue to confront the courts. More important, these problems will continue to plague growing numbers of Americans of advanced age as well as their families, dependents, and loved ones. The issue is truly one which deserves the most thorough, careful, and objective attention from all segments of society.

Weighing and then balancing a constitutionally-protected interest against the state's countervailing interests, while bearing in mind the various consequences of the decision, is quintessentially a judicial role. Despite all of the efforts of generations of courts to categorize and objectify, to create multi-part tests and identify weights to be attached to the various factors, in the end balancing entails the exercise of judicial judgment rather than the application of scientific or mathematical formulae. No legislative body can perform the task for us. Nor can any computer. In the end, mindful of our constitutional obligations, including the limitations imposed on us by that document, we must rely on our judgment, guided by the facts and the law as we perceive them.

As we have explained, in this case neither the liberty interest in choosing the time and manner of death nor the
state's countervailing interests are static. The magnitude of
each depends on objective circumstances and generally
varies inversely with the other. The liberty interest in hastening death is at its strongest when the state's interest in
protecting life and preventing suicide is at its weakest, and
vice-versa.

The liberty interest at issue here is an important one, and in
the case of the terminally ill, is at its peak. Conversely, the
state interests, while equally important in the abstract, are
for the most part at a low point here. We recognize that in
the case of life and death decisions the state has a particularly strong interest in avoiding undue influence and other
forms of abuse. Here, that concern is ameliorated in large
measure because of the mandatory involvement in the decision-making process of physicians, who have a strong bias
in favor of preserving life, and because the process itself
can be carefully regulated and rigorous safeguards adopted.
Under these circumstances, we believe that the possibility
of abuse, even when considered along with the other state
interests, does not outweigh the liberty interest at issue.

The state has chosen to pursue its interests by means of
what for terminally ill patients is effectively a total prohibition, even though its most important interests could be
adequately served by a far less burdensome measure. The
consequences of rejecting the as-applied challenge would be
disastrous for the terminally ill, while the adverse consequences for the state would be of a far lesser order. This,
too, weighs in favor of upholding the liberty interest.

We consider the state's interests in preventing assisted suicide as being different only in degree and not in kind from
its interests in prohibiting a number of other medical prac-

tices that lead directly to a terminally ill patient's death. Moreover, we do not consider those interests to be significantly greater in the case of assisted suicide than they are in the case of those other medical practices, if indeed they are greater at all. However, even if the difference were one of kind and not degree, our result would be no different. For no matter how much weight we could legitimately afford the state's interest in preventing suicide, that weight, when combined with the weight we give all the other state's interests, is insufficient to outweigh the terminally ill individual's interest in deciding whether to end his agony and suffering by hastening the time of his death with medication prescribed by his physician. The individual's interest in making that vital decision is compelling indeed, for no decision is more painful, delicate, personal, important, or final than the decision how and when one's life shall end. If broad general state policies can be used to deprive a terminally ill individual of the right to make that choice, it is hard to envision where the exercise of arbitrary and intrusive power by the state can be halted. In this case, the state has wide power to regulate, but it may not *ban* the exercise of the liberty interest, and that is the practical effect of the program before us. Accordingly, after examining one final legal authority, we hold that the "or aids" provision of Washington['s] statute is unconstitutional as applied to terminally ill competent adults who wish to hasten their deaths with medication prescribed by their physicians.

. . . . In the case before us, Chief Judge Rothstein struck down the "or aids" provision of the Washington statute as it applies to the terminally ill, not only on due process grounds but also on the ground that it violates the Equal Protection Clause. Because we are convinced that her first reason is correct, we need not consider the second. One constitutional violation is enough to support the judgment that we reach here.

We hold that a liberty interest exists in the choice of how and when one dies, and that the provision of the Washington statute banning assisted suicide, as applied to competent, terminally ill adults who wish to hasten their deaths by obtaining medication prescribed by their doctors, violates the Due Process Clause. We recognize that this decision is a most difficult and controversial one, and that it leaves unresolved a large number of equally troublesome issues that will require resolution in the years ahead. We also recognize that other able and dedicated jurists, construing the Constitution as they believe it must be construed, may disagree not only with the result we reach but with our method of constitutional analysis. Given the nature of the judicial process and the complexity of the task of determining the rights and interests comprehended by the Constitution, good faith disagreements within the judiciary should not surprise or disturb anyone who follows the development of the law. For these reasons, we express our hope that whatever debate may accompany the future exploration of the issues we have touched on today will be conducted in an objective, rational, and constructive manner that will increase, not diminish, respect for the Constitution.

There is one final point we must emphasize. Some argue strongly that decisions regarding matters affecting life or death should not be made by the courts. Essentially, we agree with that proposition. In this case, by permitting the *individual* to exercise the right to *choose* we are following the constitutional mandate to take such decisions out of the hands of the government, both state and federal, and to put them where they rightly belong, in the hands of the people. We are allowing individuals to make the decisions that so profoundly affect their very existence - and precluding the state from intruding excessively into that critical realm. The Constitution and the courts stand as a bulwark between individual freedom and arbitrary and intrusive governmental power. Under our constitutional system, neither the state nor the majority of the people in a state can impose its will upon the individual in a matter so highly "central to personal dignity and autonomy." Those who believe strongly that death must come without physician assistance are free to follow that creed, be they doctors or patients. They are not free, however, to force their views, their religious convictions, or their philosophies on all the other members of a democratic society, and to compel those whose values differ with theirs to die painful, protracted, and agonizing deaths.

[The decision of the District Court is] affirmed.

New York's Right-To-Die Decisions
Quill v. New York State Attorney General

A person is guilty of manslaughter when he intentionally aids another person to commit suicide.

- New York State's Aiding Suicide Law

On July 20, 1994 the *Quill* coalition, three terminally ill patients and their doctors, brought suit in United States District Court for the Southern District of New York against New York's Attorney General and Governor, as well as the District Attorney of New York County, seeking to have the State's criminal laws prohibiting physician-assisted suicide declared in violation of the United States Constitution.

The patients were "Jane Doe," 76 years old, dying of cancer; and George Kingsley, 48 years old, and William Barth, 28 years old, both dying of AIDS. The patients argued to the District Court that they were terminally ill, mentally competent adults who were now in the final stages of their illnesses. To avoid continued severe suffering, they had requested that their doctors assist them in committing suicide by prescribing for them lethal doses of drugs that they could self-administer. The patients, none of whom survived the litigation, asserted that they had a constitutionally protected right to physician-assisted suicide and that New York's Aiding and Promoting Suicide Laws violated their rights.

The doctors were Rochester, New York, internist, Timothy E. Quill; and New York City internists, Samuel C. Klagsbrun and Howard A. Grossman. The doctors argued to the District Court that, as their terminally ill, mentally competent patients had a constitutionally protected right to physician-assisted suicide, they had a corresponding constitutional right not to be prosecuted under New York's

Aiding and Promoting Suicide Laws for helping their patients in the exercise of these rights.

The New York State Attorney General was G. Oliver Koppell; the Governor of the State of New York was Mario Cuomo; and the District Attorney of New York County was Robert Morgenthau. The New York officials charged with enforcing the laws against aiding and promoting suicide argued to the District Court that no terminally ill, mentally competent patient had a constitutionally protected right to physician-assisted suicide and that no physician had the right to violate New York's Aiding and Promoting Suicide Laws.

New York's Aiding and Promoting Suicide Laws, which could trace their legal roots back to New York's 1828 "Self-Murder" Act, read in part: **Aiding Suicide**: "A person is guilty of manslaughter when he intentionally aids another person to commit suicide." **Promoting Suicide**: "A person is guilty of promoting a suicide attempt when he intentionally aids another person to attempt suicide." A violation of either the Aiding Suicide Law, where one person commits suicide with the assistance of another, or the Promoting Suicide law, where one person tries and fails to commit suicide with the assistance of another, was a felony punishable by imprisonment.

The *Quill* coalition based their argument for striking down New York's Aiding and Promoting Suicide Laws, as they applied to physician-assisted suicide, on two separate provisions of the United States Constitution's Fourteenth Amendment, the Due Process Clause and the Equal Protection Clause.

The Fourteenth Amendment's Due Process Clause states: "No State shall deprive any person of life, liberty, or property, without due process of law." The doctors argued that, in interpreting the Due Process Clause, the United States Supreme Court had already said in previous decisions that there were certain intimate and personal choices which were so fundamental to personal liberty (marriage, procreation, contraception, abortion, and the right to refuse medical treatment among them) that government interference was either totally prohibited or sharply limited. They believed that physician-assisted suicide was one of these constitutionally protected personal liberties.

The Fourteenth Amendment's Equal Protection Clause states: "No State shall deny to any person within its jurisdiction the equal protection of the laws." The doctors argued that if, under New York law, a competent adult could, after consulting with a doctor, legally refuse life-sustaining medical treatment, then it was a violation of the Equal Protection Clause to make it illegal to commit suicide with the aid and assistance of a doctor.

New York State, represented by their Attorney General, argued that neither the Fourteenth Amendment's Due Process nor Equal Protection Clauses overcame these important State interests in preventing the legalization of physician-assisted suicide: preserving life; preventing suicide; avoiding the involvement of third parties, and precluding the use of arbitrary, unfair, or undue influence; the effect on children, other family members, and loved ones; protecting the integrity of the medical profession; and fear of adverse consequences.

On December 15, 1994, Chief Judge Thomas Griesa of the United States District Court for the Southern District of New York issued a decision in *Quill v. New York Attorney General (Quill I)*. The Judge rejected both the doctors' due process and equal protection arguments. There existed, he ruled, no fundamental liberty to physician-assisted suicide under the Fourteenth Amendment's Due Process Clause.

Nor was there a violation of the Fourteenth Amendment's Equal Protection Clause. New York's Aiding and Promoting Suicide Laws were upheld.

The doctors appealed for a reversal of the District Court decision to the United States Court of Appeals. In the interim New York State Attorney General G. Oliver Koppell was replaced by Dennis C. Vacco and New York State Governor Mario Cuomo was replaced by George Pataki.

A three-judge appeals panel heard oral arguments from all parties on September 1, 1995 and on April 2, 1996 issued their decision in *Quill v. New York Attorney General (Quill II)*. Judge Roger Miner, writing for the Second Circuit Court of Appeals, rejected, as had the District Court, the doctors' Due Process Clause arguments. But unlike the District Court, the Court of Appeals went on to accept the doctors' Equal Protection argument, reversing the judgment of the District Court, and striking down New York's Aiding and Promoting Suicide Laws as they applied to terminally ill, mentally competent patients who would self-administer physician-prescribed lethal drugs.

The original legal text of the United States District Court's landmark right-to-die decision, *Quill v. New York Attorney General (Quill I)*, can be found in volume 870 of the *Federal Supplement*, beginning on page 78. Our plain-English edited text begins on page 143.

The original legal text of the United States Court of Appeals' landmark right-to-die decision, *Quill v. New York Attorney General (Quill II)*, can be found in volume 80 of the *Federal Reporter, 3d Series*, beginning on page 716. Our plain-English edited text begins on page 155.

Quill v. New York State Attorney General
December 15, 1994

Chief Judge Thomas Griesa: New York law makes it a crime to aid a person in committing suicide, or in attempting to commit suicide. Plaintiffs [Drs. Quill, Klagsbrun, and Grossman] urge that these provisions violate the United States Constitution, to the extent that they apply to situations where a physician aids the commission of suicide by a mentally competent, terminally ill adult wishing to avoid continued severe suffering, by prescribing a death-producing drug which the patient takes. [The doctors] claim that a person has a constitutional right to terminate his life under these circumstances, and that a physician has a corresponding constitutional right not to be prosecuted for aiding a patient in the exercise of the patient's right.

[The doctors] move for a preliminary injunction [court order stopping an action] against the enforcement of the relevant statutes of the New York Penal Law [aiding and promoting suicide], to the extent they apply to physicians who give the kind of assistance described above. [New York State] oppose[d the doctors'] motion and [moved for] dismissing the action.

. . . . The action was commenced on July 20, 1994. The original complaint named three physician[s] . . . , Timothy E. Quill, Samuel C. Klagsbrun, and Howard A. Grossman. There were also three patient[s] who asserted that they were terminally ill and wished to have the assistance of physicians in committing suicide. All three of the patient[s] have now died, leaving only the three physician[s].

. . . . The original complaint of July 20, 1994 contained, among other things, allegations that the three patient[s] were mentally competent adults; that they were in the terminal stages of fatal illnesses; that they faced progressive loss of bodily function and integrity as well as increasing suffering; and that they desired medical assistance in the form of medications prescribed by physicians to be self-administered for the purpose of hastening death.

As to the three physician[s], the complaint alleged that, in the regular course of their medical practice, they treated terminally ill patients who requested assistance in the voluntary self-termination of life; that under certain circumstances it would be consistent with the standards of these physicians to prescribe medications to such patients which would cause death, since without such medical assistance these patients could not hasten their deaths in a certain and humane manner.

The original complaint alleged that the patient[s] have a constitutional right under these circumstances to terminate their lives with this type of medical assistance; and that since the New York Penal Law makes it a crime to render such assistance, these provisions violate the constitutional rights of both the patient[s] and the physician[s], specifically rights under the Due Process and Equal Protection Clauses of the Fourteenth Amendment.

. . . . An answer was filed in August 1994 [by New York State] to the original complaint denying that [the doctors and patients] have any valid claim. . . .

The motion for preliminary injunction was filed on September 16, 1994. In support of the motion, each of the three patient[s] submitted declarations which confirmed the allegations in the complaint and added details about their diseased conditions and suffering.

The three physician[s] have submitted declarations affirming their belief that proper and humane medical practice should include the ability to prescribe medication which will enable a patient to commit suicide under the circumstances described in this case.

A declaration by Quill also describes the following incident. In 1990 he treated a terminally ill patient, who feared a lingering death and who apprised Quill that she would act on her own to hasten death if he refused to assist her to do so. Quill made barbiturates available to the patient, which she could use to induce sleep, but which she could also take to end her life by an overdose at the point she desired to do so. She agreed to meet with Quill prior to taking any overdose. The patient reached the point where she desired to end her life. She met with Quill "to insure that all alternatives had been explored," after which she took the overdose and died. Quill was not present at the time of death. Subsequently, Quill wrote an article in the New England Journal of Medicine describing these events. This led to what Quill describes as a "very public criminal investigation" in New York State, and presentation to a grand jury. Quill testified before the grand jury, as did other witnesses. The grand jury did not indict [charge with a crime].

The other two physician[s], Klagsbrun and Grossman, describe in their declarations specific incidents when terminally ill patients wished assistance in hastening death. Each doctor asserts that he refrained from rendering such assistance because of possible prosecution under the New York statutes.

[The aiding suicide s]ection . . . of the New York Penal Law provides in relevant part:

A person is guilty of manslaughter in the second
degree when . . . [h]e intentionally . . . aids another
person to commit suicide.

[The promoting suicide s]ection . . . provides:

A person is guilty of promoting a suicide attempt
when he intentionally . . . aids another person to
attempt suicide.

Violation of either statute is a felony.

[The doctors] are not seeking to strike down these statutes
in their entirety. [The doctors] claim that the statutes are
unconstitutional only insofar as they apply to the type of
physician assisted suicide at issue in this case. Both [the
doctors] and [the state] agree that, if a physician renders the
type of assistance described here, he will violate [the aiding
suicide section] where actual death by suicide occurs, and
[the promoting suicide section] where the patient attempts
to commit suicide and fails.

[The state] assert[s] that there is no justiciable case or controversy as required by Article III of the Constitution. According to [the state, the doctors] show nothing more than
a speculative possibility of prosecution.

The court does not agree with these assertions. The relevant law is well set forth. . . . [In] *Doe v. Bolton.* . . [,] a companion abortion case to *Roe v. Wade[,]* . . . the plaintiffs
challenged the Georgia anti-abortion statute. The Court
held, among other things, that the claim of the physician
plaintiffs presented a justiciable controversy. This was true
despite the fact that none of them had been prosecuted or
threatened with prosecution. The Court pointed out:

> The physician is the one against whom these criminal statutes directly operate in the event he procures an abortion that does not meet the statutory exceptions and conditions. The physician[s], therefore, assert a sufficiently direct threat of personal detriment. They should not be required to await and undergo a criminal prosecution as the sole means of seeking relief.

On the basis of these authorities, the court holds that the instant [present] case presents a justiciable controversy under Article III of the Constitution. The three physician[s] seek to carry on activities which they contend are within their constitutional rights and which would violate the New York Penal Law. This is not a case about some activity in which a plaintiff might possibly engage and which might create a hypothetical issue of criminal liability. The physician[s] credibly assert that they have had cases and continue to have cases in which their services are urgently sought to assist in the commission of suicide in the way described in this case. As to whether there is a threat of prosecution for so assisting, there has been the grand jury proceeding about . . . Quill. Although no indictment was returned, the State has by no means disavowed the intention of acting against physicians in future cases. Indeed, the State has in the present action vigorously defended its right to apply the statutes to such conduct. Thus, there is a credible threat of prosecution giving rise to sufficiently adverse positions so that a justiciable controversy exists. What is presented here is no mere abstract question.

This is particularly true since the issue of physician assisted suicide is being pressed by segments of the medical community and has sparked sharp public debate. It is most unlikely that the conduct at issue in this case would be ignored by the law enforcement authorities.

It is appropriate to note that the primary right claimed is that of the patient - i.e., the right to decide to terminate one's life and to do so by suicide. However, if such a constitutional right resides in the patient, then there would be a corresponding constitutional right of the physician not to be prosecuted for assisting in the exercise of the patient's constitutional right. The physician[s] in the present case have standing [are qualified] to raise the whole range of issues - both as to the patient's asserted right to terminate his life and the physician's right to be free from prosecution for rendering assistance.

The Fourteenth Amendment provides that no state may "deprive any person of life, liberty, or property, without due process of law." It is now established that there are certain subjects which are so fundamental to personal liberty that governmental invasion is either entirely prohibited or sharply limited. One recent articulation of this concept by the Supreme Court, which is strongly relied upon by [the doctors], is contained in the plurality opinion in *Planned Parenthood v. Casey*.

> Our law affords constitutional protection to personal decisions relating to marriage, procreation, contraception, family relationships, child rearing, and education. . . . These matters, involving the most intimate and personal choices a person may make in a lifetime, choices central to personal dignity and autonomy, are central to the liberty protected by the Fourteenth Amendment. At the heart of liberty is the right to define one's own concept of existence, of meaning, of the universe, and of the mystery of human life. Beliefs about these matters could not define the attributes of personhood were they formed under compulsion of the State.

Casey confirmed the holding in *Roe v. Wade* that the Four-teenth Amendment protects a woman's decision to abort a pregnancy in the pre-viability state.

[The doctors] also rely on the Supreme Court decision in *Cruzan v. Director, Missouri Department of Health*. In that case a woman suffered an accident, after which she could only be kept alive by artificial feeding and hydration. She lost her cognitive faculties, and apparently had no possibility of re-covery. Her parents desired to have the life-sustaining appa-ratus withdrawn. The Supreme Court of Missouri held that it was necessary, before such a step could be taken, to show by clear and convincing evidence that the injured woman would have desired withdrawal of the medical devices, and further held that such evidence was lacking.

Although the United States Supreme Court, in reviewing the case, did not provide a single convenient statement of the question before it, a fair summary of the issues would appear to be whether the injured woman had a constitu-tional right requiring the hospital to withdraw life-sustaining treatment; whether this right could be exercised on behalf of the woman by her parents; and whether the exercise of this right was unduly hampered by the evidence rule im-posed by the state court. In approaching these questions the Supreme Court stated:

> The principle that a competent person has a con-stitutionally protected liberty interest in refusing unwanted medical treatment may be inferred from our prior decisions.

The Court went on to discuss the specific issue of whether this general right to refuse treatment would apply where such refusal might lead to death.

Petitioners insist that under the general holdings of our cases, the forced administration of life-sustaining medical treatment, and even of artificially delivered food and water essential to life, would implicate a competent person's liberty interest. Although we think the logic of the cases discussed above would embrace such a liberty interest, the dramatic consequences involved in refusal of such treatment would inform the inquiry as to whether the deprivation of that interest is constitutionally permissible. But for purposes of this case, we assume that the United States Constitution would grant a competent person a constitutionally protected right to refuse lifesaving hydration and nutrition.

Thus, the Court stopped short of actually deciding that there is a constitutional right to terminate medical treatment necessary to sustain life, although the Court *assumed* the existence of such a right for the purpose of going on to the other issues in the case. As to these, the Court held that the state had the power to require evidence of the patient's wishes rather than allowing the decision solely at the behest of family members, and that the state could properly require proof of the patient's wishes by clear and convincing evidence.

[The doctors in this case] argue that the reasoning and holdings of the Supreme Court in *Roe* and *Casey* are broad enough to establish that there is a fundamental right on the part of a terminally ill patient to decide to end his life, and to do so with the type of assistance described in this case. [The doctors] also interpret the *Cruzan* decision as being tantamount to a holding that a terminally ill person has a constitutional right to require the withdrawal of life-sustaining treatment. [The doctors] argue that it follows inevitably that there is a constitutional right of physician assisted suicide under the circumstances and in the manner at issue here.

[The doctors'] reading of these cases is too broad. The Supreme Court has been careful to explain that the abortion cases, and other related decisions on procreation and child rearing, are not intended to lead automatically to the recognition of other fundamental rights on different subjects. With regard to *Cruzan,* as already described, the Court did not actually make the holding upon which [the doctors] seek to rely. In any event, it would appear clear that suicide has a sufficiently different legal significance from requesting withdrawal of treatment so that a fundamental right to suicide cannot be implied from *Cruzan.*

The Supreme Court has described the considerations which are appropriate before there can be a declaration that rights "not readily identifiable in the Constitution's text" are deserving of constitutional protection. Such rights must be implicit in the concept of ordered liberty so that neither liberty nor justice would exist if they were sacrificed. The Supreme Court has also characterized such rights as those liberties that are deeply rooted in the nation's history and traditions.

The trouble is that [the doctors] make no attempt to argue that physician assisted suicide, even in the case of terminally ill patients, has any historic recognition as a legal right. The history of the treatment of suicide by the law has been dealt with in a number of recent studies. Justice Scalia's concurring opinion in *Cruzan* also contains a useful historical summary.

Suicide was a crime under English common law, even if the motive was to avoid suffering and illness. Obviously, no punishment could be inflicted upon the deceased, but sanctions were imposed by way of forfeiture of property and ignominious burial. The American colonies apparently adopted this common law rule, but it has been gradually abandoned so that no state in this country now criminalizes suicide or attempted suicide. However, as Justice Scalia states, this change in the law resulted from a desire "to spare the innocent family and not to legitimatize the act."

As to assisting suicide, the majority of states in this country have long imposed criminal penalties on one who aids another in committing suicide. The Model Penal Code, adopted by the American Law Institute, provides that it is a crime to assist a suicide. . . . [The American Law Institute] states:

> Self destruction is surely not conduct to be encouraged or taken lightly. The fact that penal sanctions will prove ineffective to deter the suicide itself does not mean that the criminal law is equally powerless to influence the behavior of those who would aid or induce another to take his own life. Moreover, in principle it would seem that the interests in the sanctity of life that are represented by the criminal homicide laws are threatened by one who expresses a willingness to participate in taking the life of another, even though the act may be accomplished with the consent, or at the request of the suicide victim.

[The doctors] are, of course, suggesting a limited form of physician assisted suicide. But [they] have pointed to nothing in the historical record to indicate that even this form of assisted suicide has been given any kind of sanction in our legal history which will help establish it as a constitutional right.

For these reasons, the court holds that the type of physician assisted suicide at issue in this case does not involve a fundamental liberty interest protected by the Due Process Clause of the Fourteenth Amendment.

[The doctors] contend that even if there is no fundamental right to engage in assisting a patient's suicide under the Due Process Clause, they should prevail under the Equal Protection Clause. Their argument proceeds thus. It is established under New York law that a competent person may refuse medical treatment, even if the withdrawal of such treatment will result in death.

[The doctors] further argue that such refusal of treatment is essentially the same thing as committing suicide with the advice of a physician. [They] urge that for the State to sanction one course of conduct and criminalize the other involves discrimination which violates the Equal Protection Clause of the Fourteenth Amendment.

The issue is whether the distinction drawn by New York law has a reasonable and rational basis. To certain ways of thinking, there may appear to be little difference between refusing treatment in the case of a terminally ill person and taking a dose of medication which leads to death. But to another way of thinking there is a very great difference. In any event, it is hardly unreasonable or irrational for the State to recognize a difference between allowing nature to take its course, even in the most severe situations, and intentionally using an artificial death-producing device. The State has obvious legitimate interests in preserving life, and in protecting vulnerable persons. The State has the further right to determine how these crucial interests are to be treated when the issue is posed as to whether a physician can assist a patient in committing suicide. Clearly in the present public debate there are sincere and conscientious advocates for and against the concept of physician assisted suicide. Under the United States Constitution and the federal system it establishes, the resolution of this issue is left to the normal democratic processes within the State.

For these reasons the court holds that [the doctors] have not shown a violation of the Equal Protection Clause of the Fourteenth Amendment.

It should be noted that one federal district court has taken a view contrary to what is expressed in this opinion as to both the due process and the equal protection issues. [The] ruling [in *Compassion in Dying v. Washington*] is on appeal to the Ninth Circuit.

[The doctors'] motion for a preliminary injunction is denied. [New York State's] motion to dismiss . . . is granted, and the action is dismissed.

So ordered.

Quill v. New York State Attorney General
April 2, 1996

Circuit Judge Roger Miner: Plaintiff-appellants Timothy E. Quill, Samuel C. Klagsbrun and Howard A. Grossman appeal from a . . . judgment entered in the United States District Court for the Southern District of New York dismissing their . . . action against defendants-appellees [New York State Attorney General]. The action was brought by [Quill, Klagsbrun, and Grossman], all of whom are physicians, to declare unconstitutional in part two New York statutes penalizing assistance in suicide. The physicians contend that each statute is invalid to the extent that it prohibits them from acceding to the requests of terminally-ill, mentally competent patients for help in hastening death. In granting . . . judgment in favor of [the State], the district court considered and rejected challenges to the statutes predicated upon the Due Process and Equal Protection Clauses of the Fourteenth Amendment to the United States Constitution. We reverse in part, holding that physicians who are willing to do so may prescribe drugs to be self-administered to mentally competent patients who seek to end their lives during the final stages of a terminal illness.

The action giving rise to this appeal was commenced by a complaint filed on July 20, 1994. The plaintiffs named in that complaint were the three physicians who are the appellants here and three individuals then in the final stages of terminal illness: Jane Doe (who chose to conceal her actual identity), George A. Kingsley and William A. Barth. The sole defendant named in that complaint was [the New York State Attorney General]. . . . According to the complaint, Jane Doe was a 76-year-old retired physical education instructor who was dying of thyroid cancer; Mr. Kingsley was a 48-year-old publishing executive suffering from AIDS;

and Mr. Barth was a 28-year-old former fashion editor under treatment for AIDS. Each of these plaintiffs alleged that she or he had been advised and understood that she or he was in the terminal stage of a terminal illness and that there was no chance of recovery. Each sought to hasten death "in a certain and humane manner" and for that purpose sought "necessary medical assistance in the form of medications prescribed by [her or his] physician to be self-administered."

The [doctors] alleged that they encountered, in the course of their medical practices, "mentally competent, terminally ill patients who request assistance in the voluntary self-termination of life." Many of these patients apparently "experience chronic, intractable pain and/or intolerable suffering" and seek to hasten their deaths for those reasons. Mr. Barth was one of the patients who sought the assistance of Dr. Grossman. Each of the physician[s] has alleged that "[u]nder certain circumstances it would be consistent with the standards of [his] medical practice" to assist in hastening death by prescribing drugs for patients to self-administer for that purpose. The physicians alleged that they were unable to exercise their best professional judgment to prescribe the requested drugs, and the [patients] alleged that they were unable to receive the requested drugs, because of the prohibitions contained in sections 125.15(3) and 120.30 of the New York Penal Law, all plaintiffs being residents of New York.

Section 125.15 of the New York Penal Law provides in pertinent part:

> A person is guilty of manslaughter in the second degree when . . . [h]e intentionally . . . aids another person to commit suicide.

A violation of this provision is classified as a class C felony.

Section 120.30 of the New York Penal Law provides:

> A person is guilty of promoting a suicide attempt when he intentionally . . . aids another person to attempt suicide.

A violation of this provision is classified as a class E felony.

Count I of the [doctors'] complaint included an allegation that "[t]he Fourteenth Amendment guarantees the liberty of mentally competent, terminally ill adults with no chance of recovery to make decisions about the end of their lives." It also included an allegation that

> [t]he Fourteenth Amendment guarantees the liberty of physicians to practice medicine consistent with their best professional judgment, including using their skills and powers to facilitate the exercise of the decision of competent, terminally ill adults to hasten inevitable death by prescribing suitable medications for the patient to self-administer for that purpose.

Count II of the complaint included an allegation that

> [t]he relevant portions of . . . the New York Penal Law deny the patient-plaintiffs and the patients of the physician-plaintiffs the equal protection of the law by denying them the right to choose to hasten inevitable death, while terminally ill persons whose treatment includes life support are able to exercise this choice with necessary medical assistance by directing termination of such treatment.

In their [request] for relief the [doctors] requested judgment declaring the New York statutes complained of constitutionally invalid and therefore in violation of [the U.S. Code] "as applied to physicians who assist mentally competent, terminally ill adults who choose to hasten inevitable death." [The doctors] also sought an order permanently enjoining [stopping] [the State] from enforcing the statutes. . . .

By order to show cause filed on September 16, 1994, the [doctors] moved for a preliminary injunction [court order] to enjoin [stop New York State's Attorney General] "and all persons acting in concert and participation with him" from enforcing [the] New York Penal Law [aiding and promoting suicide] against physicians who prescribe medications which mentally competent, terminally ill patients may use to hasten their impending deaths." A declaration by each of the plaintiffs was submitted in support of the application, although Jane Doe had died prior to the filing of the order to show cause. Plaintiffs Kingsley and Barth were then in the advanced stages of AIDS and therefore sought an immediate determination by the district court.

In her declaration, Jane Doe stated:

> I have a large cancerous tumor which is wrapped around the right carotid artery in my neck and is collapsing my esophagus and invading my voice box. The tumor has significantly reduced my ability to swallow and prevents me from eating anything but very thin liquids in extremely small amounts. The cancer has metastasized to my plural [sic] cavity and it is painful to yawn or cough. . . . In early July 1994 I had the [feeding] tube implanted and have suffered serious problems as a result. . . . I take a variety of medications to manage the pain. . . . It is not possible for me to re-

duce my pain to an acceptable level of comfort and to retain an alert state. . . . At this time, it is clear to me, based on the advice of my doctors, that I am in the terminal phase of this disease. . . . At the point at which I can no longer endure the pain and suffering associated with my cancer, I want to have drugs available for the purpose of hastening my death in a humane and certain manner. I want to be able to discuss freely with my treating physician my intention of hastening my death through the consumption of drugs prescribed for that purpose.

Mr. Kingsley subscribed to a declaration that included the following:

At this time I have almost no immune system function. . . . My first major illness associated with AIDS was cryptosporidiosis, a parasitic infection which caused me severe fevers and diarrhea and associated pain, suffering and exhaustion. . . . I also suffer from cytomegalovirus ("CMV") retinitis, an AIDS-related virus which attacks the retina and causes blindness. To date I have become almost completely blind in my left eye. I am at risk of losing my sight altogether from this condition. . . . I also suffer from toxoplasmosis, a parasitic infection which has caused lesions to develop on my brain. . . . I . . . take daily infusions of cytovene for the . . . retinitis condition. This medication, administered for an hour through a Hickman tube which is connected to an artery in my chest, prevents me from ever taking showers and makes simple routine functions burdensome. In addition, I inject my leg daily with neupogen to combat the deficient white cell count in my blood. The daily injection of this medication is extremely painful. ... At this point it is clear to me, based on the advice of my doctors, that I am in the terminal phase of [AIDS]. ... It is my desire that my physician prescribe suitable drugs for me to consume for the purpose of hastening my death when and if my suffering becomes intolerable.

In his declaration, Mr. Barth stated:

In May 1992, I developed a Kaposi's sarcoma skin lesion. This was my first major illness associated with AIDS. I underwent radiation and chemotherapy to treat this cancer. ... In September 1993, I was diagnosed with cytomegalovirus ("CMV") in my stomach and colon which caused severe diarrhea, fevers and wasting. ... In February 1994, I was diagnosed with microsporidiosis, a parasitic infection for which there is effectively no treatment. ... At approximately the same time, I contracted AIDS-related pneumonia. The pneumonia's infusion therapy treatment was so extremely toxic that I vomited with each infusion. ... In March 1994, I was diagnosed with cryptosporidiosis, a parasitic infection which has caused severe diarrhea, sometimes producing 20 stools a day, extreme abdominal pain, nausea and additional significant wasting. I have begun to lose bowel control. ... For each of these conditions I have undergone a variety of medical treatments, each of which has had significant adverse side effects. ... While I have tolerated some [nightly intravenous] feedings, I am unwilling to accept this for an extended period of time. ... I understand that there are no cures. ... I can no longer endure the pain and suffering . . . and I want to have drugs available for the purpose of hastening my death.

. . . . Supplemental declarations in support of the [doctors'] motion for preliminary injunction also were filed on October 14, 1994. In their supplemental declarations, Doctors Klagsbrun and Grossman reiterated their desire "to prescribe drugs, if and when medically and psychiatrically appropriate, for such patients to self-administer at the time and place of their choice for the purpose of hastening their impending deaths."

In his supplemental declaration, Dr. Quill declared:

The removal of a life support system that directly results in the patient's death requires the direct involvement by the doctor, as well as other medical personnel. When such patients are mentally competent, they are consciously choosing death as preferable to life under the circumstances that they are forced to live. Their doctors do a careful clinical assessment, including a full exploration of the patient's prognosis, mental competence to make such decisions, and the treatment alternatives to stopping treatment. It is legally and ethically permitted for physicians to actively assist patients to die who are dependent on life-sustaining treatments. . . . Unfortunately, some dying patients who are in agony that can no longer be relieved, yet are not dependent on life-sustaining treatment, have no such options under current legal restrictions. It seems unfair, discriminatory, and inhumane to deprive some dying patients of such vital choices because of arbitrary elements of their condition which determine whether they are on life-sustaining treatment that can be stopped.

Along with the supplemental declarations filed on October 14th, an original declaration in support of the motion was filed by Dr. Jack Froom, a physician and Professor of Family Medicine with substantial experience in detecting depression in primary care patients. He declared:

> Physicians can determine whether a patient's request to hasten death is rational and competent or motivated by depression or other mental illness or instability. Physicians currently make these determinations as to patient capacity to make end-of-life decisions with respect to orders not to resuscitate and refusal of life-sustaining treatment. . . . Terminally ill persons who seek to hasten death by consuming drugs need medical counseling regarding the type of drugs and the amount and manner in which they should be taken, as well as a prescription, which only a licensed medical doctor can provide. . . . Knowing what drug, in what amount, will hasten death for a particular patient, in light of the patient's medical condition and medication regimen, is a complex medical task. . . . It is not uncommon, in light of present legal constraints on physician assistance, that patients seeking to hasten their death try to do so without medical advice. . . . Very often, patients who survive a failed suicide attempt find themselves in worse condition than before the attempt. Brain damage, for example, is one result of failed suicide attempts.

. . . . These patients, according to the physicians, understood "their condition, diagnosis, and prognosis and wish[ed] to avoid prolonged suffering by hastening their deaths if and when their suffering [became] intolerable." None of the three terminally-ill [patients] named in the original complaint survived to the date of the district court's decision.

The opinion of the district court was filed on December 16, 1994. The district court denied the motion for a preliminary injunction and granted the [State's] . . . motion to dismiss the action. . . . After finding that the action presented a justiciable case or controversy, the district court first addressed the due process issue. The court determined that physician assisted suicide could not be classified as a fundamental right within the meaning of the Constitution:

> The Supreme Court has described the considerations which are appropriate before there can be a declaration that rights "not readily identifiable in the Constitution's text" are deserving of constitutional protection. Such rights must be implicit in the concept of ordered liberty so that neither liberty nor justice would exist if they were sacrificed. The Supreme Court has also characterized such rights as those liberties that are deeply rooted in the nation's history and traditions.

> The trouble is that plaintiffs make no attempt to argue that physician assisted suicide, even in the case of terminally ill patients, has any historic recognition as a legal right.

Accordingly, the district court concluded "that the type of physician assisted suicide at issue in this case does not involve a fundamental liberty interest protected by the Due Process Clause of the Fourteenth Amendment."

Turning to the equal protection issue, the district court identified a reasonable and rational basis for the distinction drawn by New York law between the refusal of treatment at the hands of physicians and physician assisted suicide:

> [I]t is hardly unreasonable or irrational for the State to recognize a difference between allowing nature to take its course, even in the most severe situations, and intentionally using an artificial death-producing device. The State has obvious legitimate interests in preserving life, and in protecting vulnerable persons. The State has the further right to determine how these crucial interests are to be treated when the issue is posed as to whether a physician can assist a patient in committing suicide.

Accordingly, the court held "that plaintiffs have not shown a violation of the Equal Protection Clause of the Fourteenth Amendment."

As they did in the district court, [New York State] contend[s] on appeal that this action does not present a justiciable case or controversy. We reject this contention.

. . . . The Court in *Doe [v. Bolton]* held that plaintiff physicians had presented a justiciable controversy despite the fact that none had been threatened with prosecution. The law that the physicians challenged was a criminal statute that directly criminalized the physician's participation in abortion. Accordingly, a sufficiently concrete controversy was presented.

The same principles lead to the conclusion that there is a case or controversy at issue here. Dr. Quill has had a criminal proceeding instituted against him in the past, and the state nowhere disclaims an intent to repeat a prosecution in the event of further assisted suicides. The other two physician plaintiffs also face the threat of criminal prosecution. Like the physicians in *Doe*, they "should not be required to await and undergo a criminal prosecution as the sole means of seeking relief." Finally, under *Doe*, the physicians may raise the rights of their terminally-ill patients.

Although [New York County] District Attorney Morgenthau argues in his brief on appeal that appellants [the doctors] have not shown that they are in any jeopardy of prosecution in New York County, a recent indictment [charge] by a New York County grand jury demonstrates the contrary. A newspaper report printed on December 15, 1995 disclosed the following:

> Yesterday, [the] District Attorney . . . of Manhattan announced that a grand jury had indicted [George] Delury, an editor who lives on the Upper West Side, on manslaughter charges for helping his 52-year-old wife, Myrna Lebov, commit suicide last summer.

The physician[s] have good reason to fear prosecution in New York County.

[The doctors] argue for a right to assisted suicide as a fundamental liberty under the substantive component of the Due Process Clause of the Fourteenth Amendment. This Clause assures the citizenry that any deprivation of life, liberty or property by a state will be attended by appropriate legal processes. However,

> despite the language of the Due Process Clause . . . , which appears to focus only on the processes by which life, liberty, or property is taken, the cases are legion in which th[at] Clause [has] been interpreted to have substantive content, subsuming rights that

to a great extent are immune from . . . state regulation or proscription. Among such cases are those recognizing rights that have little or no textual support in the constitutional language.

Rights that have no textual support in the language of the Constitution but qualify for heightened judicial protection include fundamental liberties so "implicit in the concept of ordered liberty" that "neither liberty nor justice would exist if they were sacrificed." Fundamental liberties also have been described as those that are "deeply rooted in this Nation's history and tradition." It is well settled that the state must not infringe fundamental liberty interests unless the infringement is narrowly tailored to serve a compelling state interest. The list of rights the Supreme Court has actually or impliedly identified as fundamental, and therefore qualified for heightened judicial protection, include the fundamental guarantees of the Bill of Rights as well as the following: freedom of association; the right to participate in the electoral process and to vote; the right to travel interstate; the right to fairness in the criminal process; the right to procedural fairness in regard to claims for governmental deprivations of life, liberty or property; and the right to privacy. The right to privacy has been held to encompass personal decisions relating to marriage, procreation, family relationships, child rearing and education, contraception and abortion. While the Constitution does not, of course, include any explicit mention of the right of privacy, this right has been recognized as encompassed by the Fourteenth Amendment's Due Process Clause. Nevertheless, the Supreme Court has been reluctant to further expand this particular list of federal rights, and it would be most speculative for a lower court to do so.

In any event, the Supreme Court has drawn a line, albeit a shaky one, on the expansion of fundamental rights that are without support in the text of the Constitution. In *Bowers*, the Supreme Court framed the issue as "whether the Federal Constitution confers a fundamental right upon homosexuals to engage in sodomy and hence invalidates the laws of the many States that still make such conduct illegal and have done so for a very long time." Holding that there was no fundamental right to engage in consensual sodomy, the Court noted that the statutes proscribing such conduct had "ancient roots." The Court noted that sodomy was a common law criminal offense, forbidden by the laws of the original thirteen states when they ratified the Bill of Rights, and that twenty-five states and the District of Columbia still penalize sodomy performed in private by consenting adults.

As in *Bowers*, the statutes [the doctors] seek to declare unconstitutional here cannot be said to infringe upon any fundamental right or liberty. As in *Bowers*, the right contended for here cannot be considered so implicit in our understanding of ordered liberty that neither justice nor liberty would exist if it were sacrificed. Nor can it be said that the right to assisted suicide claimed by [the doctors] is deeply rooted in the nation's traditions and history. Indeed, the very opposite is true. The Common Law of England, as received by the American colonies, prohibited suicide and attempted suicide. Although neither suicide nor attempted suicide is any longer a crime in the United States, thirty-two states, including New York, continue to make assisted suicide an offense. Clearly, no "right" to assisted suicide ever has been recognized in any state in the United States.

In rejecting the due process-fundamental rights argument of the [doctors], we are mindful of the admonition of the Supreme Court:

> Nor are we inclined to take a more expansive view
> of our authority to discover new fundamental

rights imbedded in the Due Process Clause. The Court is most vulnerable and comes nearest to illegitimacy when it deals with judge-made constitutional law having little or no cognizable roots in the language or design of the Constitution.

The right to assisted suicide finds no cognizable basis in the Constitution's language or design, even in the very limited cases of those competent persons who, in the final stages of terminal illness, seek the right to hasten death. We therefore decline the plaintiffs' invitation to identify a new fundamental right, in the absence of a clear direction from the Court whose precedents we are bound to follow. The limited room for expansion of substantive due process rights and the reasons therefor have been clearly stated: "As a general matter, the [U.S. Supreme] Court has always been reluctant to expand the concept of substantive due process because guideposts for responsible decisionmaking in this uncharted area are scarce and open-ended." Our position in the judicial hierarchy constrains us to be even more reluctant than the Court to undertake an expansive approach in this uncharted area.

According to the Fourteenth Amendment, the equal protection of the laws cannot be denied by any State to any person within its jurisdiction. This constitutional guarantee simply requires the states to treat in a similar manner all individuals who are similarly situated. But disparate treatment is not necessarily a denial of the equal protection guaranteed by the Constitution. The Supreme Court has described the wide discretion afforded to the states in establishing acceptable classifications:

> The Equal Protection Clause directs that "all persons similarly circumstanced shall be treated alike." But so too, "[t]he Constitution does not require

things which are different in fact or opinion to be
treated in law as though they were the same." The
initial discretion to determine what is "different"
and what is "the same" resides in the legislatures
of the States. A legislature must have substantial
latitude to establish classifications that roughly ap-
proximate the nature of the problem perceived,
that accommodate competing concerns both public and private, and that account for limitations on
the practical ability of the State to remedy every ill.
In applying the Equal Projection Clause to most
forms of state action, we thus seek only the assurance that the classification at issue bears some fair
relationship to a legitimate public purpose.

. . . . Applying the foregoing principles to the New York
statutes criminalizing assisted suicide, it seems clear that: 1)
the statutes in question fall within the category of social
welfare legislation and therefore are subject to rational basis
scrutiny upon judicial review; 2) New York law does not
treat equally all competent persons who are in the final
stages of fatal illness and wish to hasten their deaths; 3) the
distinctions made by New York law with regard to such
persons do not further any legitimate state purpose; and 4)
accordingly, to the extent that the statutes in question prohibit persons in the final stages of terminal illness from
having assistance in ending their lives by the use of self-
administered, prescribed drugs, the statutes lack any rational
basis and are violative of the Equal Protection Clause.

The right to refuse medical treatment long has been recognized in New York. In 1914 Judge Cardozo wrote that, under New York law, "[e]very human being of adult years and
sound mind has a right to determine what shall be done
with his own body." In 1981, the New York Court of Appeals held that this right extended to the withdrawal of life-

support systems. The *Eichner* case involved a terminally-ill, 83-year-old patient whose guardian ultimately was authorized to withdraw the patient's respirator. The [New York] Court of Appeals determined that the guardian had proved by clear and convincing evidence that the patient, prior to becoming incompetent due to illness, had consistently expressed his view that life should not be prolonged if there was no hope of recovery. In *Storar,* the companion case to *Eichner,* the Court of Appeals determined that a profoundly retarded, terminally-ill patient was incapable of making a decision to terminate blood transfusions. There, the patient was incapable of making a reasoned decision, having never been competent at any time in his life. In both these cases, the New York Court of Appeals recognized the right of a competent, terminally-ill patient to hasten his death upon proper proof of his desire to do so.

The [New York] Court of Appeals revisited the issue in *Rivers v. Katz.* In that case, the Court recognized the right to bring on death by refusing medical treatment not only as a "fundamental common-law right" but also as "coextensive with [a] patient's liberty interest protected by the due process clause of our State Constitution." The following language was included in the opinion:

> In our system of a free government, where notions of individual autonomy and free choice are cherished, it is the individual who must have the final say in respect to decisions regarding his medical treatment in order to insure that the greatest possible protection is accorded his autonomy and freedom from unwanted interference with the furtherance of his own desires.

After these cases were decided, the [legislature] placed its imprimatur upon the right of competent citizens to hasten death by refusing medical treatment and by directing physicians to remove life-support systems already in place. In 1987, the legislature enacted Article 29-B of the New York Public Health Law, entitled "Orders Not to Resuscitate." The Article provides that an "adult with capacity" may direct the issuance of an order not to resuscitate. . . .

In 1990, the New York legislature enacted Article 29-C of the Public Health Law, entitled "Health Care Agents and Proxies." This statute allows for a person to sign a health care proxy, for the purpose of appointing an agent with "authority to make any and all health care decisions on the principal's behalf that the principal could make." These decisions include those relating to the administration of artificial nutrition and hydration, provided the wishes of the principal are known to the agent. . . .

The concept that a competent person may order the removal of life-support systems found [U.S.] Supreme Court approval in *Cruzan*. . . . There the Court upheld a determination of the Missouri Supreme Court that required proof by clear and convincing evidence of a patient's desire for the withdrawal of life-sustaining equipment. The patient in that case, Nancy Cruzan, was in a persistent vegetative state as the result of injuries sustained in an automobile accident. Her parents sought court approval in the State of Missouri to terminate the artificial nutrition and hydration with which she was supplied at the state hospital where she was confined. The hospital employees refused to withdraw the life-support systems, without which Cruzan would suffer certain death. The trial court authorized the withdrawal after finding that Cruzan had expressed some years before to a housemate friend some thoughts that suggested she would not wish to live on a life-support system. The trial court also found that one in Cruzan's condition had a fundamental right to refuse death-prolonging procedures.

The Missouri Supreme Court, in reversing the trial court, refused to find a broad right of privacy in the state constitution that would support a right to refuse treatment. Moreover, that court doubted that such a right existed under the United States Constitution. It did identify a state policy in the Missouri Living Will Statute favoring the preservation of life and concluded that, in the absence of compliance with the statute's formalities or clear and convincing evidence of the patient's choice, no person could order the withdrawal of medical life-support services.

In affirming [upholding] the Missouri Supreme Court, the United States Supreme Court stated: "The principle that a competent person has a constitutionally protected liberty interest in refusing unwanted medical treatment may be inferred from our prior decisions." The Court noted that the inquiry is not ended by the identification of a liberty interest, because there also must be a balancing of the state interests and the individual's liberty interests before there can be a determination that constitutional rights have been violated. The Court all but made that determination in the course of the following analysis:

> Petitioners insist that under the general holdings of our cases, the forced administration of life-sustaining medical treatment, and even of artificially-delivered food and water essential to life, would implicate a competent person's liberty interest. Although we think the logic of the cases discussed above would embrace such a liberty interest, the dramatic consequences involved in refusal of such treatment would inform the inquiry as to whether the deprivation of that interest is constitutionally permissible. But for purposes of this case, we assume that the United States Con-

stitution would grant a competent person a constitutionally protected right to refuse lifesaving hydration and nutrition.

The Court went on to find that Missouri allowed a surrogate to "act for the patient in electing to have hydration and
nutrition withdrawn in such a way as to cause death," subject to "a procedural safeguard to assure that the action of
the surrogate conforms as best it may to the wishes expressed by the patient while competent." The Court then
held that the procedural safeguard or requirement imposed
by Missouri - the heightened evidentiary requirement that
the incompetent's wishes be proved by clear and convincing evidence - was not forbidden by the United States Constitution.

In view of the foregoing, it seems clear that New York does
not treat similarly circumstanced persons alike: those in the
final stages of terminal illness who are on life-support systems are allowed to hasten their deaths by directing the removal of such systems; but those who are similarly situated,
except for the previous attachment of life-sustaining
equipment, are not allowed to hasten death by self-
administering prescribed drugs. The district judge has identified "a difference between allowing nature to take its
course, even in the most severe situations, and intentionally
using an artificial death-producing device." But Justice
Scalia, for one, has remarked upon "the irrelevance of the
action-inaction distinction," noting that "the cause of death
in both cases is the suicide's conscious decision to 'pu[t] an
end to his own existence.'"

Indeed, there is nothing "natural" about causing death by
means other than the original illness or its complications.
The withdrawal of nutrition brings on death by starvation,
the withdrawal of hydration brings on death by dehydra-

tion, and the withdrawal of ventilation brings about respiratory failure. By ordering the discontinuance of these artificial life-sustaining processes or refusing to accept them in the first place, a patient hastens his death by means that are not natural in any sense. It certainly cannot be said that the death that immediately ensues is the natural result of the progression of the disease or condition from which the patient suffers.

Moreover, the writing of a prescription to hasten death, after consultation with a patient, involves a far less active role for the physician than is required in bringing about death through asphyxiation, starvation and/or dehydration. Withdrawal of life-support requires physicians or those acting at their direction physically to remove equipment and, often, to administer palliative drugs which may themselves contribute to death. The ending of life by these means is nothing more nor less than assisted suicide. It simply cannot be said that those mentally competent, terminally-ill persons who seek to hasten death but whose treatment does not include life support are treated equally.

A finding of unequal treatment does not, of course, end the inquiry, unless it is determined that the inequality is not rationally related to some legitimate state interest. The burden is upon the [doctors] to demonstrate irrationality. At oral argument and in its brief, the state's contention has been that its principal interest is in preserving the life of all its citizens at all times and under all conditions. But what interest can the state possibly have in requiring the prolongation of a life that is all but ended? Surely, the state's interest lessens as the potential for life diminishes. And what business is it of the state to require the continuation of agony when the result is imminent and inevitable? What concern prompts the state to interfere with a mentally competent patient's "right to define [his] own concept of existence, of meaning, of the universe, and of the mystery of human life," when the patient seeks to have drugs prescribed to end life during the final stages of a terminal illness? The greatly reduced interest of the state in preserving life compels the answer to these questions: "None."

A panel of the Ninth Circuit attempted to identify some state interests in reversing a district court decision holding unconstitutional a statute of the State of Washington criminalizing the promotion of a suicide attempt. The plaintiffs in the Washington case contended for physician-assisted suicide for the terminally-ill, but the panel majority found that the statute prohibiting suicide promotion furthered the following: the interest in denying to physicians "the role of killers of their patients"; the interest in avoiding psychological pressure upon the elderly and infirm to consent to death; the interest of preventing the exploitation of the poor and minorities; the interest in protecting handicapped persons against societal indifference; the interest in preventing the sort of abuse that "has occurred in the Netherlands where . . . legal guidelines have tacitly allowed assisted suicide or euthanasia in response to a repeated request from a suffering, competent patient." The panel majority also raised a question relative to the lack of clear definition of the term "terminally ill."

The New York statutes prohibiting assisted suicide, which are similar to the Washington statute, do not serve any of the state interests noted, in view of the statutory and common law schemes allowing suicide through the withdrawal of life-sustaining treatment. Physicians do not fulfill the role of "killer" by prescribing drugs to hasten death any more than they do by disconnecting life-support systems. Likewise, "psychological pressure" can be applied just as much upon the elderly and infirm to consent to withdrawal of life-sustaining equipment as to take drugs to hasten death.

There is no clear indication that there has been any problem in regard to the former, and there should be none as to the latter. In any event, the state of New York may establish rules and procedures to assure that all choices are free of such pressures. With respect to the protection of minorities, the poor and the non-mentally handicapped, it suffices to say that these classes of persons are entitled to treatment equal to that afforded to all those who now may hasten death by means of life-support withdrawal. In point of fact, these persons *themselves* are entitled to hasten death by requesting such withdrawal and should be free to do so by requesting appropriate medication to terminate life during the final stages of terminal illness.

As to the interest in avoiding abuse similar to that occurring in the Netherlands, it seems clear that some physicians there practice nonvoluntary euthanasia, although it is not legal to do so. The [doctors] here do not argue for euthanasia at all but for assisted suicide for terminally-ill, mentally competent patients, who would self-administer the lethal drugs. It is difficult to see how the relief the [doctors] seek would lead to the abuses found in the Netherlands. Moreover, note should be taken of the fact that the Royal Dutch Medical Association recently adopted new guidelines for those physicians who choose to accede to the wishes of patients to hasten death. Under the new guidelines, patients must self-administer drugs whenever possible, and physicians must obtain a second opinion from another physician who has no relationship with the requesting physician or his patient.

Finally, it seems clear that most physicians would agree on the definition of "terminally ill," at least for the purpose of the relief that [the doctors] seek. The [doctors] seek to hasten death only where a patient is in the "final stages" of "terminal illness," and it seems even more certain that physicians would agree on when this condition occurs. Physicians are accustomed to advising patients and their families in this regard and frequently do so when decisions are to be made regarding the furnishing or withdrawal of life-support systems. Again, New York may define that stage of illness with greater particularity, require the opinion of more than one physician or impose any other obligation upon patients and physicians who collaborate in hastening death.

The New York statutes criminalizing assisted suicide violate the Equal Protection Clause because, to the extent that they prohibit a physician from prescribing medications to be self-administered by a mentally competent, terminally-ill person in the final stages of his terminal illness, they are not rationally related to any legitimate state interest.

We reverse the judgment of the district court. . . .

The Supreme Court's Landmark Decision In Washington's Right-To-Die Case
Washington State v. Glucksberg

January 29, 1994. A coalition of physicians (including Dr. Harold Glucksberg), terminally ill patients, and a right-to-die advocacy group files suit in U.S. District Court, challenging the constitutionality of Washington's Promoting Suicide Law as it applies specifically to physician-assisted suicide. The challenged statute, with roots going back to 1854, reads: *A person is guilty of promoting a suicide attempt when he knowingly causes or aids another person to attempt suicide.* The case is called *Compassion in Dying v. Washington State.*

May 3, 1994. Judge Barbara Rothstein issues a decision in *Compassion in Dying I.* Washington's Promoting Suicide Law as it applies specifically to physician-assisted suicide is held to be a violation of both the Fourteenth Amendment's Due Process and Equal Protection Clauses. Judge Rothstein writes: *A competent, terminally ill adult has a constitutionally guaranteed right under the Fourteenth Amendment to commit physician-assisted suicide.* Washington State appeals to a three-judge panel of the Ninth Circuit Court of Appeals for a reversal of this decision.

March 9, 1995. A three-judge panel of the Ninth Circuit Court of Appeals issues a decision in *Compassion in Dying II.* Washington State's Promoting Suicide Law as it applies specifically to physician-assisted suicide is held not to violate either the Fourteenth Amendment's Due Process or Equal Protection Clauses. Judge John T. Noonan, Jr. writes: *In the two hundred and five years of our existence no constitutional right to aid in killing oneself has ever been asserted and upheld by a court of final jurisdiction.* The *Compassion in Dying* coalition appeals to the full Ninth Circuit Court of Appeals for a reversal of this decision.

March 6, 1996. The full Ninth Circuit Court of Appeals issues a decision in *Compassion in Dying III.* Washington State's Promoting Suicide Law as it applies specifically to physician-assisted suicide is held to be in violation of the Fourteenth Amendment's Due Process Clause. Judge Stephen Reinhardt writes: *Those who believe strongly that death must come without physician assistance are free to follow that creed, be they doctors or patients. They are not free, however, to force their views, their religious convictions, or their philosophies on all the other members of a democratic society, and to compel those whose values differ with theirs to die painful, protracted, and agonizing deaths.* Washington State appeals to the U.S. Supreme Court for a reversal of this decision. The case is renamed *Washington State v. Glucksberg.*

January 8, 1997. The U.S. Supreme Court hears oral arguments. Speaking for Washington, Assistant Attorney General William Williams argues: *The issue here today is whether the Constitution requires that the social policy developed by Washington voters must be supplanted by a far different social policy, a constitutionally recognized right to physician-assisted suicide that is contrary to our traditions and overrides the important state interests that are served by the Washington statute.* Speaking for Glucksberg, Kathryn Tucker argues: *This case presents the question whether dying citizens in full possession of their mental faculties at the threshold of death due to terminal illness have the liberty to choose to cross that threshold in a humane and dignified manner.*

June 26, 1997. The United States Supreme Court issues a unanimous decision in *Washington State v. Glucksberg.* Washington State's Promoting Suicide Law as it applies specifically to physician-assisted suicide is held not to violate the Fourteenth Amendment's Due Process Clause.

The original legal text of the United States Supreme Court's landmark decision in *Washington State v. Glucksberg* can be found in volume 521 of *United States Reports.* Our plain-English edited text begins on page 181.

WASHINGTON STATE
v. GLUCKSBERG
June 26, 1997

Chief Justice William Rehnquist: The question presented in this case is whether Washington's prohibition against "caus[ing]" or "aid[ing]" a suicide offends the Fourteenth Amendment to the United States Constitution. We hold that it does not.

It has always been a crime to assist a suicide in the State of Washington. In 1854, Washington's first Territorial Legislature outlawed "assisting another in the commission of self-murder." Today, Washington law provides: "A person is guilty of promoting a suicide attempt when he knowingly causes or aids another person to attempt suicide." "Promoting a suicide attempt" is a felony, punishable by up to five years' imprisonment and up to a $10,000 fine. At the same time, Washington's Natural Death Act, enacted in 1979, states that the "withholding or withdrawal of life-sustaining treatment" at a patient's direction "shall not, for any purpose, constitute a suicide."

Petitioners in this case are the State of Washington and its Attorney General. Respondents Harold Glucksberg, M. D., Abigail Halperin, M. D., Thomas A. Preston, M. D., and Peter Shalit, M. D., are physicians who practice in Washington. These doctors occasionally treat terminally ill, suffering patients, and declare that they would assist these patients in ending their lives if not for Washington's assisted-suicide ban. In January 1994, [the doctors], along with three gravely ill, pseudonymous plaintiffs who have since died and Compassion in Dying, a nonprofit organization that counsels people considering physician-assisted suicide, sued in the United States District Court, seeking a declaration that [the Washington law prohibiting physician-assisted suicide] is . . . unconstitutional.

The plaintiffs asserted "the existence of a liberty interest protected by the Fourteenth Amendment which extends to a personal choice by a mentally competent, terminally ill adult to commit physician-assisted suicide." Relying primarily on *Planned Parenthood v. Casey* and *Cruzan v. Director, Missouri Dept. of Health,* the District Court agreed, and concluded that Washington's assisted-suicide ban is unconstitutional because it "places an undue burden on the exercise of [that] constitutionally protected liberty interest." The District Court also decided that the Washington statute violated the Equal Protection Clause's requirement that "'all persons similarly situated . . . be treated alike.'"

A panel of the Court of Appeals for the Ninth Circuit reversed, emphasizing that "[i]n the two hundred and five years of our existence no constitutional right to aid in killing oneself has ever been asserted and upheld by a court of final jurisdiction." The Ninth Circuit reheard the case en banc [with the entire court participating in the decision], reversed the panel's decision, and affirmed [upheld] the District Court. Like the District Court, the en banc Court of Appeals emphasized our Casey and Cruzan decisions. The court also discussed what it described as "historical" and "current societal attitudes" toward suicide and assisted suicide, and concluded that "the Constitution encompasses a due process liberty interest in controlling the time and manner of one's death - that there is, in short, a constitutionally-recognized right to die. After "[w]eighing and then balancing" this interest against Washington's various interests, the court held that the State's assisted-suicide ban was unconstitutional "as applied to terminally ill competent adults who wish to hasten their deaths with medication prescribed by their physicians." The court did not reach the District Court's equal-protection holding. We granted certiorari [agreed to hear the case], and now reverse.

We begin, as we do in all due-process cases, by examining our Nation's history, legal traditions, and practices. In almost every State - indeed, in almost every western democracy - it is a crime to assist a suicide. The States' assisted-suicide bans are not innovations. Rather, they are longstanding expressions of the States' commitment to the protection and preservation of all human life. Indeed, opposition to and condemnation of suicide - and, therefore, of assisting suicide - are consistent and enduring themes of our philosophical, legal, and cultural heritages.

More specifically, for over 700 years, the Anglo-American common-law tradition [law established by usage] has punished or otherwise disapproved of both suicide and assisting suicide. In the 13th century, Henry de Bracton, one of the first legal-treatise writers, observed that "[j]ust as a man may commit felony by slaying another so may he do so by slaying himself." The real and personal property of one who killed himself to avoid conviction and punishment for a crime were forfeit to the king; however, thought Bracton, "if a man slays himself in weariness of life or because he is unwilling to endure further bodily pain ... [only] his movable goods [were] confiscated." Thus, "[t]he principle that suicide of a sane person, for whatever reason, was a punishable felony was ... introduced into English common law." Centuries later, Sir William Blackstone, whose *Commentaries on the Laws of England* not only provided a definitive summary of the common law but was also a primary legal authority for 18th and 19th century American lawyers, referred to suicide as "self-murder" and "the pretended heroism, but real cowardice, of the Stoic philosophers, who destroyed themselves to avoid those ills which they had not the fortitude to endure . . . ." Blackstone emphasized that "the law has . . . ranked [suicide] among the highest crimes," although, anticipating later developments, he conceded that the harsh and shameful punishments imposed for suicide "borde[r] a little upon severity."

For the most part, the early American colonies adopted the common-law approach. For example, the legislators of the Providence Plantations, which would later become Rhode Island, declared, in 1647, that "[s]elf-murder is by all agreed to be the most unnatural, and it is by this present Assembly declared, to be that, wherein he that doth it, kills himself out of a premeditated hatred against his own life or other humor: . . . his goods and chattels are the king's custom, but not his debts nor lands; but in case he be an infant, a lunatic, mad or distracted man, he forfeits nothing." Virginia also required ignominious burial for suicides, and their estates were forfeit to the crown.

Over time, however, the American colonies abolished these harsh common-law penalties. William Penn abandoned the criminal-forfeiture sanction in Pennsylvania in 1701, and the other colonies (and later, the other States) eventually followed this example. Zephaniah Swift, who would later become Chief Justice of Connecticut, wrote in 1796 that

> "[t]here can be no act more contemptible, than to attempt to punish an offender for a crime, by exercising a mean act of revenge upon lifeless clay, that is insensible of the punishment. There can be no greater cruelty, than the inflicting [of] a punish-

ment, as the forfeiture of goods, which must fall solely on the innocent offspring of the offender.... [Suicide] is so abhorrent to the feelings of mankind, and that strong love of life which is implanted in the human heart, that it cannot be so frequently committed, as to become dangerous to society. There can of course be no necessity of any punishment."

This statement makes it clear, however, that the movement away from the common law's harsh sanctions did not represent an acceptance of suicide; rather, as Chief Justice Swift observed, this change reflected the growing consensus that it was unfair to punish the suicide's family for his wrongdoing. Nonetheless, although States moved away from Blackstone's treatment of suicide, courts continued to condemn it as a grave public wrong.

That suicide remained a grievous, though nonfelonious, wrong is confirmed by the fact that colonial and early state legislatures and courts did not retreat from prohibiting assisting suicide. Swift, in his early 19th century treatise on the laws of Connecticut, stated that "[i]f one counsels another to commit suicide, and the other by reason of the advice kills himself, the advisor is guilty of murder as principal." This was the well established common-law view, as was the similar principle that the consent of a homicide victim is "wholly immaterial to the guilt of the person who cause[d] [his death]." And the prohibitions against assisting suicide never contained exceptions for those who were near death. Rather, "[t]he life of those to whom life ha[d] become a burden - of those who [were] hopelessly diseased or fatally wounded - nay, even the lives of criminals condemned to death, [were] under the protection of law, equally as the lives of those who [were] in the full tide of life's enjoyment, and anxious to continue to live."

The earliest American statute explicitly to outlaw assisting suicide was enacted in New York in 1828, and many of the new States and Territories followed New York's example. Between 1857 and 1865, a New York commission led by Dudley Field drafted a criminal code that prohibited "aiding" a suicide and, specifically, "furnish[ing] another person with any deadly weapon or poisonous drug, knowing that such person intends to use such weapon or drug in taking his own life." By the time the Fourteenth Amendment was ratified, it was a crime in most States to assist a suicide. The Field Penal Code was adopted in the Dakota Territory in 1877, in New York in 1881, and its language served as a model for several other western States' statutes in the late 19th and early 20th centuries. California, for example, codified its assisted-suicide prohibition in 1874, using language similar to the Field Code's. In this century, the Model Penal Code also prohibited "aiding" suicide, prompting many States to enact or revise their assisted-suicide bans. The Code's drafters observed that "the interests in the sanctity of life that are represented by the criminal homicide laws are threatened by one who expresses a willingness to participate in taking the life of another, even though the act may be accomplished with the consent, or at the request, of the suicide victim."

Though deeply rooted, the States' assisted-suicide bans have in recent years been reexamined and, generally, reaffirmed. Because of advances in medicine and technology, Americans today are increasingly likely to die in institutions, from chronic illnesses. Public concern and democratic action are therefore sharply focused on how best to protect dignity and independence at the end of life, with the result that there have been many significant changes in state laws and in the attitudes these laws reflect. Many States, for example, now permit "living wills," surrogate health-care decisionmaking, and the withdrawal or refusal of life-sustaining medical treatment. At the same time, however, voters and legislators continue for the most part to reaffirm their States' prohibitions on assisting suicide.

The Washington statute at issue in this case was enacted in 1975 as part of a revision of that State's criminal code. Four years later, Washington passed its Natural Death Act, which specifically stated that the "withholding or withdrawal of life-sustaining treatment . . . shall not, for any purpose, constitute a suicide" and that "[n]othing in this chapter shall be construed [interpreted] to condone, authorize, or approve mercy killing . . . ." In 1991, Washington voters rejected a ballot initiative which, had it passed, would have permitted a form of physician-assisted suicide. Washington then added a provision to the Natural Death Act expressly excluding physician-assisted suicide.

California voters rejected an assisted-suicide initiative similar to Washington's in 1993. On the other hand, in 1994, voters in Oregon enacted, also through ballot initiative, that State's "Death With Dignity Act," which legalized physician-assisted suicide for competent, terminally ill adults. Since the Oregon vote, many proposals to legalize assisted-suicide have been and continue to be introduced in the States' legislatures, but none has been enacted. And just last year, Iowa and Rhode Island joined the overwhelming majority of States explicitly prohibiting assisted suicide. Also, on April 30, 1997, President Clinton signed the Federal Assisted Suicide Funding Restriction Act of 1997, which prohibits the use of federal funds in support of physician-assisted suicide.

Thus, the States are currently engaged in serious, thoughtful examinations of physician-assisted suicide and other similar issues. For example, New York State's Task Force on Life and the Law - an ongoing, blue-ribbon commission composed of doctors, ethicists, lawyers, religious leaders, and interested laymen - was convened in 1984 and commissioned with "a broad mandate to recommend public policy on issues raised by medical advances." Over the past decade, the Task Force has recommended laws relating to end-of-life decisions, surrogate pregnancy, and organ donation. After studying physician-assisted suicide, however, the Task Force unanimously concluded that "[l]egalizing assisted suicide and euthanasia would pose profound risks to many individuals who are ill and vulnerable. . . . [T]he potential dangers of this dramatic change in public policy would outweigh any benefit that might be achieved."

Attitudes toward suicide itself have changed since Bracton, but our laws have consistently condemned, and continue to prohibit, assisting suicide. Despite changes in medical technology and notwithstanding an increased emphasis on the importance of end-of-life decisionmaking, we have not retreated from this prohibition. Against this backdrop of history, tradition, and practice, we now turn to respondents' constitutional claim.

The Due Process Clause guarantees more than fair process, and the "liberty" it protects includes more than the absence of physical restraint. The Clause also provides heightened protection against government interference with certain fundamental rights and liberty interests. In a long line of cases, we have held that, in addition to the specific freedoms protected by the Bill of Rights, the "liberty" specially protected by the Due Process Clause includes the rights to marry; to have children; to direct the education and upbringing of one's children; to marital privacy; to use contraception; to bodily integrity; and to abortion. We have also assumed, and strongly suggested, that the Due Process Clause protects the traditional right to refuse unwanted lifesaving medical treatment.

But we "ha[ve] always been reluctant to expand the concept of substantive due process because guideposts for responsible decisionmaking in this uncharted area are scarce and open-ended." By extending constitutional protection to an asserted right or liberty interest, we, to a great extent, place the matter outside the arena of public debate and legislative action. We must therefore "exercise the utmost care whenever we are asked to break new ground in this field," lest the liberty protected by the Due Process Clause be subtly transformed into the policy preferences of the members of this Court.

Our established method of substantive-due-process analysis has two primary features: First, we have regularly observed that the Due Process Clause specially protects those fundamental rights and liberties which are, objectively, "deeply rooted in this Nation's history and tradition," and "implicit in the concept of ordered liberty," such that "neither liberty nor justice would exist if they were sacrificed." Second, we have required in substantive-due-process cases a "careful description" of the asserted fundamental liberty interest. Our Nation's history, legal traditions, and practices thus provide the crucial "guideposts for responsible decisionmaking" that direct and restrain our exposition of the Due Process Clause. As we stated recently in *[Reno v.]*

Flores, the Fourteenth Amendment "forbids the government to infringe . . . 'fundamental' liberty interests at all, no
matter what process is provided, unless the infringement is
narrowly tailored to serve a compelling state interest."

. . . . Turning to the claim at issue here, the Court of
Appeals stated that "[p]roperly analyzed, the first issue to
be resolved is whether there is a liberty interest in determining the time and manner of one's death," or, in other
words, "[i]s there a right to die?" Similarly, respondents
assert a "liberty to choose how to die" and a right to
"control of one's final days," and describe the asserted
liberty as "the right to choose a humane, dignified death,"
and "the liberty to shape death." As noted above, we have a
tradition of carefully formulating the interest at stake in
substantive-due-process cases. For example, although
Cruzan is often described as a "right to die" case, we were,
in fact, more precise: we assumed that the Constitution
granted competent persons a "constitutionally protected
right to refuse lifesaving hydration and nutrition." The
Washington statute at issue in this case prohibits "aid[ing]
another person to attempt suicide," and, thus, the question
before us is whether the "liberty" specially protected by the
Due Process Clause includes a right to commit suicide
which itself includes a right to assistance in doing so.

We now inquire whether this asserted right has any place in
our Nation's traditions. Here, as discussed above, we are
confronted with a consistent and almost universal tradition
that has long rejected the asserted right, and continues
explicitly to reject it today, even for terminally ill, mentally
competent adults. To hold for respondents, we would have
to reverse centuries of legal doctrine and practice, and
strike down the considered policy choice of almost every
State.

Respondents contend, however, that the liberty interest they assert is consistent with this Court's substantive-due-process line of cases, if not with this Nation's history and practice. Pointing to *Casey* and *Cruzan*, respondents read our jurisprudence in this area as reflecting a general tradition of "self-sovereignty," and as teaching that the "liberty" protected by the Due Process Clause includes "basic and intimate exercises of personal autonomy." According to respondents, our liberty jurisprudence, and the broad, individualistic principles it reflects, protects the "liberty of competent, terminally ill adults to make end-of-life decisions free of undue government interference." The question presented in this case, however, is whether the protections of the Due Process Clause include a right to commit suicide with another's assistance. With this "careful description" of respondents' claim in mind, we turn to *Casey* and *Cruzan*.

In *Cruzan*, we considered whether Nancy Beth Cruzan, who had been severely injured in an automobile accident and was in a persistent vegetative state, "ha[d] a right under the United States Constitution which would require the hospital to withdraw life-sustaining treatment" at her parents' request. We began with the observation that "[a]t common law, even the touching of one person by another without consent and without legal justification was a battery." We then discussed the related rule that "informed consent is generally required for medical treatment." After reviewing a long line of relevant state cases, we concluded that "the common-law doctrine of informed consent is viewed as generally encompassing the right of a competent individual to refuse medical treatment." Next, we reviewed our own cases on the subject, and stated that "[t]he principle that a competent person has a constitutionally protected liberty interest in refusing unwanted medical treatment may be inferred from our prior decisions." Therefore, "for purposes of [that] case, we assume[d] that the United States Constitution would grant a competent person a constitutionally protected right to refuse lifesaving hydration and nutrition." We concluded that, notwithstanding this right, the Constitution permitted Missouri to require clear and convincing evidence of an incompetent patient's wishes concerning the withdrawal of life-sustaining treatment.

Respondents contend that in *Cruzan* we "acknowledged that competent, dying persons have the right to direct the removal of life-sustaining medical treatment and thus hasten death," and that "the constitutional principle behind recognizing the patient's liberty to direct the withdrawal of artificial life support applies at least as strongly to the choice to hasten impending death by consuming lethal medication." Similarly, the Court of Appeals concluded that "*Cruzan*, by recognizing a liberty interest that includes the refusal of artificial provision of life-sustaining food and water, necessarily recognize[d] a liberty interest in hastening one's own death."

The right assumed in *Cruzan*, however, was not simply deduced from abstract concepts of personal autonomy. Given the common-law rule that forced medication was a battery, and the long legal tradition protecting the decision to refuse unwanted medical treatment, our assumption was entirely consistent with this Nation's history and constitutional traditions. The decision to commit suicide with the assistance of another may be just as personal and profound as the decision to refuse unwanted medical treatment, but it has never enjoyed similar legal protection. Indeed, the two acts are widely and reasonably regarded as quite distinct. In *Cruzan* itself, we recognized that most

States outlawed assisted suicide - and even more do today - and we certainly gave no intimation that the right to refuse unwanted medical treatment could be somehow transmuted into a right to assistance in committing suicide.

Respondents also rely on *Casey*. There, the Court's opinion concluded that "the essential holding of *Roe v. Wade* should be retained and once again reaffirmed." We held, first, that a woman has a right, before her fetus is viable, to an abortion "without undue interference from the State"; second, that States may restrict post-viability abortions, so long as exceptions are made to protect a woman's life and health; and third, that the State has legitimate interests throughout a pregnancy in protecting the health of the woman and the life of the unborn child. In reaching this conclusion, the opinion discussed in some detail this Court's substantive-due-process tradition of interpreting the Due Process Clause to protect certain fundamental rights and "personal decisions relating to marriage, procreation, contraception, family relationships, child rearing, and education," and noted that many of those rights and liberties "involv[e] the most intimate and personal choices a person may make in a lifetime."

The Court of Appeals, like the District Court, found *Casey* "highly instructive" and "almost prescriptive" for determining "'what liberty interest may inhere in a terminally ill person's choice to commit suicide'":

> "Like the decision of whether or not to have an abortion, the decision how and when to die is one of 'the most intimate and personal choices a person may make in a lifetime,' a choice 'central to personal dignity and autonomy.'"

Similarly, respondents emphasize the statement in *Casey* that:

> "At the heart of liberty is the right to define one's own concept of existence, of meaning, of the universe, and of the mystery of human life. Beliefs about these matters could not define the attributes of personhood were they formed under compulsion of the State."

By choosing this language, the Court's opinion in *Casey* described, in a general way and in light of our prior cases, those personal activities and decisions that this Court has identified as so deeply rooted in our history and traditions, or so fundamental to our concept of constitutionally ordered liberty, that they are protected by the Fourteenth Amendment. The opinion moved from the recognition that liberty necessarily includes freedom of conscience and belief about ultimate considerations to the observation that "though the abortion decision may originate within the zone of conscience and belief, it is more than a philosophic exercise." That many of the rights and liberties protected by the Due Process Clause sound in personal autonomy does not warrant the sweeping conclusion that any and all important, intimate, and personal decisions are so protected, and *Casey* did not suggest otherwise.

The history of the law's treatment of assisted suicide in this country has been and continues to be one of the rejection of nearly all efforts to permit it. That being the case, our decisions lead us to conclude that the asserted "right" to assistance in committing suicide is not a fundamental liberty interest protected by the Due Process Clause. The Constitution also requires, however, that Washington's assisted-suicide ban be rationally related to legitimate government interests. This requirement is unquestionably met here. As the court below [the Court of Appeals] recognized, Washington's assisted-suicide ban implicates a number of state interests.

First, Washington has an "unqualified interest in the preservation of human life." The State's prohibition on assisted suicide, like all homicide laws, both reflects and advances its commitment to this interest. This interest is symbolic and aspirational as well as practical:

> "While suicide is no longer prohibited or penalized, the ban against assisted suicide and euthanasia shores up the notion of limits in human relationships. It reflects the gravity with which we view the decision to take one's own life or the life of another, and our reluctance to encourage or promote these decisions."

> Respondents admit that "[t]he State has a real interest in preserving the lives of those who can still contribute to society and enjoy life." The Court of Appeals also recognized Washington's interest in protecting life, but held that the "weight" of this interest depends on the "medical condition and the wishes of the person whose life is at stake." Washington, however, has rejected this sliding-scale approach and, through its assisted-suicide ban, insists that all persons' lives, from beginning to end, regardless of physical or mental condition, are under the full protection of the law. As we have previously affirmed, the States "may properly decline to make judgments about the 'quality' of life that a particular individual may

enjoy." This remains true, as *Cruzan* makes clear, even for those who are near death.

Relatedly, all admit that suicide is a serious public-health problem, especially among persons in otherwise vulnerable groups. The State has an interest in preventing suicide, and in studying, identifying, and treating its causes.

Those who attempt suicide - terminally ill or not - often suffer from depression or other mental disorders. Research indicates, however, that many people who request physician-assisted suicide withdraw that request if their depression and pain are treated. The New York Task Force, however, expressed its concern that, because depression is difficult to diagnose, physicians and medical professionals often fail to respond adequately to seriously ill patients' needs. Thus, legal physician-assisted suicide could make it more difficult for the State to protect depressed or mentally ill persons, or those who are suffering from untreated pain, from suicidal impulses.

The State also has an interest in protecting the integrity and ethics of the medical profession. In contrast to the Court of Appeals' conclusion that "the integrity of the medical profession would [not] be threatened in any way by [physician-assisted suicide]," the American Medical Association, like many other medical and physicians' groups, has concluded that "[p]hysician-assisted suicide is fundamentally incompatible with the physician's role as healer." And physician-assisted suicide could, it is argued, undermine the trust that is essential to the doctor-patient relationship by blurring the time-honored line between healing and harming.

Next, the State has an interest in protecting vulnerable groups - including the poor, the elderly, and disabled persons - from abuse, neglect, and mistakes. The Court of Appeals dismissed the State's concern that disadvantaged persons might be pressured into physician-assisted suicide as "ludicrous on its face." We have recognized, however, the real risk of subtle coercion and undue influence in end-of-life situations. Similarly, the New York Task Force warned that "[l]egalizing physician-assisted suicide would pose profound risks to many individuals who are ill and vulnerable. . . . The risk of harm is greatest for the many individuals in our society whose autonomy and well-being are already compromised by poverty, lack of access to good medical care, advanced age, or membership in a stigmatized social group." If physician-assisted suicide were permitted, many might resort to it to spare their families the substantial financial burden of end-of-life health-care costs.

The State's interest here goes beyond protecting the vulnerable from coercion; it extends to protecting disabled and terminally ill people from prejudice, negative and inaccurate stereotypes, and "societal indifference." The State's assisted-suicide ban reflects and reinforces its policy that the lives of terminally ill, disabled, and elderly people must be no less valued than the lives of the young and healthy, and that a seriously disabled person's suicidal impulses should be interpreted and treated the same way as anyone else's.

Finally, the State may fear that permitting assisted suicide will start it down the path to voluntary and perhaps even involuntary euthanasia. The Court of Appeals struck down Washington's assisted-suicide ban only "as applied to competent, terminally ill adults who wish to hasten their deaths by obtaining medication prescribed by their doctors." Washington insists, however, that the impact of the court's decision will not and cannot be so limited. If suicide is protected as a matter of constitutional right, it is argued, "every man and woman in the United States must enjoy it." The Court of Appeals' decision, and its expansive reasoning, provide ample support for the State's concerns. The court noted, for example, that the "decision of a duly appointed surrogate decision maker is for all legal purposes the decision of the patient himself"; that "in some instances, the patient may be unable to self-administer the drugs and . . . administration by the physician . . . may be the only way the patient may be able to receive them"; and that not only physicians, but also family members and loved ones, will inevitably participate in assisting suicide. Thus, it turns out that what is couched as a limited right to "physician-assisted suicide" is likely, in effect, a much broader license, which could prove extremely difficult to police and contain. Washington's ban on assisting suicide prevents such erosion.

This concern is further supported by evidence about the practice of euthanasia in the Netherlands. The Dutch government's own study revealed that in 1990, there were 2,300 cases of voluntary euthanasia (defined as "the deliberate termination of another's life at his request"), 400 cases of assisted suicide, and more than 1,000 cases of euthanasia without an explicit request. In addition to these latter 1,000 cases, the study found an additional 4,941 cases where physicians administered lethal morphine overdoses without the patients' explicit consent. This study suggests that, despite the existence of various reporting procedures, euthanasia in the Netherlands has not been limited to competent, terminally ill adults who are enduring physical suffering, and that regulation of the practice may not have prevented abuses in cases involving vulnerable persons, including severely disabled neonates and elderly persons suffering from dementia. The New York Task Force, citing the Dutch experience, observed that "assisted suicide and euthanasia are closely linked," and concluded that the "risk of . . . abuse is neither speculative nor distant." Washington, like most other States, reasonably ensures against this risk by banning, rather than regulating, assisting suicide.

We need not weigh exactingly the relative strengths of these various interests. They are unquestionably important and legitimate, and Washington's ban on assisted suicide is at least reasonably related to their promotion and protection. We therefore hold that [the Washington statute prohibiting physician-assisted suicide] does not violate the Fourteenth Amendment . . . "as applied to competent, terminally ill adults who wish to hasten their deaths by obtaining medication prescribed by their doctors."

Throughout the Nation, Americans are engaged in an earnest and profound debate about the morality, legality, and practicality of physician-assisted suicide. Our holding permits this debate to continue, as it should in a democratic society. The decision of the en banc Court of Appeals is reversed, and the case is remanded [sent back to the lower court] for further proceedings consistent with this opinion.

It is so ordered.

The Supreme Court's Landmark Decision In New York's Right-To-Die Case
New York State v. Quill

July 20, 1994. A coalition of physicians (including Dr. Timothy Quill) and terminally ill patients files suit in U.S. District Court against New York State, challenging the constitutionality of New York's Aiding and Promoting Suicide Laws as they apply specifically to physician-assisted suicide. The challenged statutes, with roots going back to 1828, read: *A person is guilty of manslaughter when he intentionally aids another person to commit suicide. A person is guilty of promoting a suicide attempt when he intentionally aids another person to attempt suicide.* The case is called *Quill v. New York State.*

December 15, 1994. Judge Thomas Griesa issues a decision in *Quill I.* New York State's Aiding and Promoting Suicide Laws as they apply specifically to physician-assisted suicide are held not to violate either the Fourteenth Amendment's Due Process or Equal Protection Clauses. Judge Griesa writes: *It is hardly unreasonable or irrational for [New York] State to recognize a difference between allowing nature to take its course, even in the most severe situations, and intentionally using an artificial death-producing device.* The *Quill* coalition appeals to the Second Circuit Court of Appeals for a reversal of this decision.

April 2, 1996. The Second Circuit Court of Appeals issues a decision in *Quill II.* New York State's Aiding and Promoting Suicide Laws as they apply specifically to physician-assisted suicide are held to violate the Fourteenth Amendment's Equal Protection Clause. Judge Roger Miner writes: *The New York statutes criminalizing assisted suicide violate the Equal Protection Clause because, to the extent that they prohibit a physician from prescribing medications to be self-administered by a mentally competent, terminally-ill person in the final stages of his terminal illness, they are not rationally related to any legitimate state interest.*

New York State appeals to the U.S. Supreme Court for a reversal of this decision.

January 8, 1997. The U.S. Supreme Court hears oral arguments in *New York State v. Quill.* Speaking for New York State, State Attorney General Dennis Vacco argues: *The question in this case is whether the State must remain neutral in the face of a decision of one of its citizens to help another kill herself. The [United States Court of Appeals for the] Second Circuit said "Yes" as a matter of equal protection. It is New York's view, however, that the Constitution does not require this to be the case.* Speaking for Quill, Harvard Law Professor Lawrence Tribe argues: *The liberty interest in this case is the liberty, when facing imminent and inevitable death, not to be forced by the government to endure a degree of pain and suffering that one can relieve only by being completely unconscious. Not to be forced into that choice, that the liberty is the freedom, at this threshold at the end of life, not to be a creature of the state but to have some voice in the question of how much pain one is really going through.*

June 26, 1997. The United States Supreme Court issues a unanimous decision in *New York State v. Quill.* New York's Aiding and Promoting Suicide Laws as they apply specifically to physician-assisted suicide are held not to violate the Fourteenth Amendment's Equal Protection Clause.

The original legal text of the United States Supreme Court's landmark decision in *New York State v. Quill* can be found in volume 521 of *United States Reports.* Our plain-English edited text begins on page 203.

NEW YORK STATE v. QUILL
June 26, 1997

Chief Justice William Rehnquist: In New York, as in most States, it is a crime to aid another to commit or attempt suicide, but patients may refuse even lifesaving medical treatment. The question presented by this case is whether New York's prohibition on assisting suicide therefore violates the Equal Protection Clause of the Fourteenth Amendment. We hold that it does not.

Petitioners are various New York public officials. Respondents Timothy E. Quill, Samuel C. Klagsbrun, and Howard A. Grossman are physicians who practice in New York. They assert that although it would be "consistent with the standards of [their] medical practice[s]" to prescribe lethal medication for "mentally competent, terminally ill patients" who are suffering great pain and desire a doctor's help in taking their own lives, they are deterred from doing so by New York's ban on assisting suicide. Respondents, and three gravely ill patients who have since died, sued the State's Attorney General in the United States District Court. They urged that because New York permits a competent person to refuse life-sustaining medical treatment, and because the refusal of such treatment is "essentially the same thing" as physician-assisted suicide, New York's assisted-suicide ban violates the Equal Protection Clause.

The District Court disagreed: "[I]t is hardly unreasonable or irrational for the State to recognize a difference between allowing nature to take its course, even in the most severe situations, and intentionally using an artificial death-producing device." The court noted New York's "obvious legitimate interests in preserving life, and in protecting vulnerable persons," and concluded that "[u]nder the United States Constitution and the federal system it establishes, the resolution of this issue is left to the normal democratic processes within the State."

The Court of Appeals for the Second Circuit reversed. The court determined that, despite the assisted-suicide ban's apparent general applicability, "New York law does not treat equally all competent persons who are in the final stages of fatal illness and wish to hasten their deaths," because "those in the final stages of terminal illness who are on life-support systems are allowed to hasten their deaths by directing the removal of such systems; but those who are similarly situated, except for the previous attachment of life-sustaining equipment, are not allowed to hasten death by self-administering prescribed drugs." In the court's view, "[t]he ending of life by [the withdrawal of life-support systems] is nothing more nor less than assisted suicide." The Court of Appeals then examined whether this supposed unequal treatment was rationally related to any legitimate state interests, and concluded that "to the extent that [New York's statutes] prohibit a physician from prescribing medications to be self-administered by a mentally competent, terminally-ill person in the final stages of his terminal illness, they are not rationally related to any legitimate state interest." We granted certiorari [agreed to hear the case], and now reverse.

The Equal Protection Clause commands that no State shall "deny to any person within its jurisdiction the equal protection of the laws." This provision creates no substantive rights. Instead, it embodies a general rule that States must treat like cases alike but may treat unlike cases accordingly. If a legislative classification or distinction "neither burdens a fundamental right nor targets a suspect class, we will uphold [it] so long as it bears a rational relation to some legitimate end."

New York's statutes outlawing assisting suicide affect and address matters of profound significance to all New Yorkers alike. They neither infringe fundamental rights nor involve suspect classifications. These laws are therefore entitled to a "strong presumption of validity."

. . . [N]either New York's ban on assisting suicide nor its statutes permitting patients to refuse medical treatment treat anyone differently than anyone else or draw any distinctions between persons. *Everyone*, regardless of physical condition, is entitled, if competent, to refuse unwanted lifesaving medical treatment; *no one* is permitted to assist a suicide. Generally speaking, laws that apply evenhandedly to all "unquestionably comply" with the Equal Protection Clause.

The Court of Appeals, however, concluded that some terminally ill people - those who are on life-support systems - are treated differently than those who are not, in that the former may "hasten death" by ending treatment, but the latter may not "hasten death" through physician-assisted suicide. This conclusion depends on the submission that ending or refusing lifesaving medical treatment "is nothing more nor less than assisted suicide." Unlike the Court of Appeals, we think the distinction between assisting suicide and withdrawing life-sustaining treatment, a distinction widely recognized and endorsed in the medical profession and in our legal traditions, is both important and logical; it is certainly rational.

The distinction comports with fundamental legal principles of causation and intent. First, when a patient refuses life-sustaining medical treatment, he dies from an underlying fatal disease or pathology; but if a patient ingests lethal medication prescribed by a physician, he is killed by that medication.

Furthermore, a physician who withdraws, or honors a patient's refusal to begin life-sustaining medical treatment purposefully intends, or may so intend, only to respect his patient's wishes and "to cease doing useless and futile or degrading things to the patient when [the patient] no longer stands to benefit from them." The same is true when a doctor provides aggressive palliative care; in some cases, painkilling drugs may hasten a patient's death, but the physician's purpose and intent is, or may be, only to ease his patient's pain. A doctor who assists a suicide, however, "must, necessarily and indubitably, intend primarily that the patient be made dead." Similarly, a patient who commits suicide with a doctor's aid necessarily has the specific intent to end his or her own life, while a patient who refuses or discontinues treatment might not.

The law has long used actors' intent or purpose to distinguish between two acts that may have the same result. Put differently, the law distinguishes actions taken "because of" a given end from actions taken "in spite of" their unintended but foreseen consequences.

Given these general principles, it is not surprising that many courts, including New York courts, have carefully distinguished refusing life-sustaining treatment from suicide. In fact, the first state-court decision explicitly to authorize withdrawing lifesaving treatment noted the "real distinction between the self-infliction of deadly harm and a self-determination against artificial life support." And recently, the Michigan Supreme Court also rejected the argument that the distinction "between acts that artificially sustain life and acts that artificially curtail life" is merely a "distinction without constitutional significance - a meaningless exercise in semantic gymnastics," insisting that "the *Cruzan* majority disagreed and so do we."

Similarly, the overwhelming majority of state legislatures have drawn a clear line between assisting suicide and withdrawing or permitting the refusal of unwanted lifesaving medical treatment by prohibiting the former and permitting the latter. And "nearly all states expressly disapprove of suicide and assisted suicide either in statutes dealing with durable powers of attorney in health-care situations, or in 'living will' statutes." Thus, even as the States move to protect and promote patients' dignity at the end of life, they remain opposed to physician-assisted suicide.

New York is a case in point. The State enacted its current assisted-suicide statutes in 1965. Since then, New York has acted several times to protect patients' common-law [law established by usage and tradition] right to refuse treatment. In so doing, however, the State has neither endorsed a general right to "hasten death" nor approved physician-assisted suicide. Quite the opposite: The State has reaffirmed the line between "killing" and "letting die." More recently, the New York State Task Force on Life and the Law studied assisted suicide and euthanasia and, in 1994, unanimously recommended against legalization. In the Task Force's view, "allowing decisions to forego life-sustaining treatment and allowing assisted suicide or euthanasia have radically different consequences and meanings for public policy."

This Court has also recognized, at least implicitly, the distinction between letting a patient die and making that patient die. In *Cruzan v. Director, Missouri Dept. of Health,* we concluded that "[t]he principle that a competent person has a constitutionally protected liberty interest in refusing unwanted medical treatment may be inferred from our prior decisions," and we assumed the existence of such a right for purposes of that case. But our assumption of a right to refuse treatment was grounded not, as the Court of Appeals supposed, on the proposition that patients have a general and abstract "right to hasten death," but on well established, traditional rights to bodily integrity and freedom from unwanted touching. In fact, we observed that "the majority of States in this country have laws imposing criminal penalties on one who assists another to commit suicide." *Cruzan* therefore provides no support for the notion that refusing life-sustaining medical treatment is "nothing more nor less than suicide."

For all these reasons, we disagree with respondents' claim that the distinction between refusing lifesaving medical treatment and assisted suicide is "arbitrary" and "irrational." Granted, in some cases, the line between the two may not be clear, but certainty is not required, even were it possible. Logic and contemporary practice support New York's judgment that the two acts are different, and New York may therefore, consistent with the Constitution, treat them differently. By permitting everyone to refuse unwanted medical treatment while prohibiting anyone from assisting a suicide, New York law follows a longstanding and rational distinction.

New York's reasons for recognizing and acting on this distinction - including prohibiting intentional killing and preserving life; preventing suicide; maintaining physicians' role as their patients' healers; protecting vulnerable people from indifference, prejudice, and psychological and financial pressure to end their lives; and avoiding a possible slide towards euthanasia - are discussed in greater detail in our opinion in *Glucksberg*. These valid and important public interests easily satisfy the constitutional requirement that a legislative classification bear a rational relation to some legitimate end.

The judgment of the Court of Appeals is reversed.

It is so ordered.

Bibliography

Alvarez, A. *The Savage God: A Study of Suicide.* New York,
NY: Bantam Books, 1996.

Baird, Robert M., and Stuart E. Rosenbaum, Editors.
Euthanasia: The Moral Issues. Buffalo, NY: Prometheus
Books, 1993.

Barnard, Christian. *Good Life Good Death: A Doctor's Case for
Euthanasia and Suicide.* New York, NY: Prentice-Hall, 1980.

Barry, Robert L. *Breaking the Thread of Life: On Rational
Suicide.* New Brunswick, NJ: Transaction Publishers, 1994.

Basta, Lofty, and Carol Post. *A Graceful Exit: Life and Death
on Your Own Terms.* New York, NY: Insight Books, 1996.

Bell, Reed, and Frank York. *Prescription Death: Compassionate
Killers in the Medical Profession.* Lafayette, LA: Huntington
House, 1993.

Beltran, Joseph E. *The Living Will and Other Life-and-Death
Medical Choices.* Nashville, TN: Nelson, 1994.

Beauchamp, Tom L., Editor. *Intending Death: The Ethics of
Assisted Suicide and Euthanasia.* Upper Saddle River, NJ:
Prentice-Hall, 1996.

Beauchamp, Tom L., et al. *Matters of Life and Death.*
Philadelphia, PA: Temple University Press, 1980.

Brody, Baruch A. *Life and Death Decisionmaking.* New York,
NY: Oxford University Press, 1988.

Burnell, George M. *Final Choices: To Live or To Die in an Age of Medical Technology*. New York, NY: Insight Books, 1993.

Cantor, Norman L. *Advance Directives and the Pursuit of Death with Dignity*. Bloomington, IN: Indiana University Press, 1993.

_____. *Legal Frontiers of Death and Dying*. Bloomington, IN: Indiana University Press, 1987.

Christner, Anne M., Editor. *End-Of-Life Decisions: Facing the Challenges of Medical and Ethical Choices*. Providence, RI: Manisses Communications, 1996.

Clark, Nina. *The Politics of Physician-Assisted Suicide*. New York, NY: Garland, 1997.

Colt, George H. *The Enigma of Suicide*. New York, NY: Simon & Schuster, 1991.

Cox, Donald W. *Hemlock's Cup: The Struggle for Death with Dignity*. Buffalo, NY: Prometheus Books, 1993.

Cundiff, David. *Euthanasia is Not the Answer: A Hospice Physician's View*. Totowa, NJ: Humana Press, 1992.

DeSimone, Cathleen. *Death on Demand: Physician-Assisted Suicide in the United States*. Buffalo, NY: W.S. Hein, 1996.

Downing, A.B., Editor. *Euthanasia and the Right to Death: The Case for Voluntary Euthanasia*. New York, NY: Humanities Press, 1970.

Flanders, Stephen A. *Suicide*. New York, NY: Facts on File, 1991.

Fruehling, James A., Editor. *Sourcebook on Death and Dying.* Chicago, IL: Marquis Professional Publications, 1982.

Grisez, Germain, and Joseph M. Boyle, Jr. *Life and Death with Liberty and Justice: A Contribution to the Euthanasia Debate.* Notre Dame, IN: University of Notre Dame Press, 1980.

Hamel, Ronald P., and Edwin R. DuBose, Editors. *Must We Suffer Our Way To Death? Cultural and Theological Perspectives on Death by Choice.* Dallas, TX: Southern Methodist University Press, 1996.

Heofler, James M. *Deathright: Culture, Medicine, Politics and the Right to Die.* Boulder, CO: Westview Press, 1994.

Hill, T. Patrick, Editor, and David Shirley. *A Good Death: Taking More Control At The End Of Your Life.* Reading, MA: Addison-Wesley Publishing Co., 1992.

Hilton, Bruce. *First, Do No Harm: Wrestling with the New Medicine's Life and Death Dilemmas.* Nashville, TN: Abingdon, 1991.

Horan, Dennis J., and David Mall, editors. *Death, Dying, and Euthanasia.* Westport, CT: Greenwood Press, 1980.

Humber, James M., et al., Editors. *Physician-Assisted Death.* Totowa, NJ: Humana Press, 1993.

Humphry, Derek. *Assisted Suicide: The Compassionate Crime.* Los Angeles, CA: Hemlock Society, 1984.

_____. *Dying with Dignity: Understanding Euthanasia.* New York, NY: Carol Publishing, 1992.

214 Life, Death, and the Law

_____. *Final Exit: The Practicalities of Self-Deliverance and Assisted Suicide.* Eugene, OR: Hemlock Society, 1991.

_____. *Lawful Exit: The Limits of Freedom for Help in Dying.* Junction City, OR: Norris Lane Press, 1993.

_____, and Ann Wickett. *The Right to Die: Understanding Euthanasia.* New York, NY: Harper & Row, 1986.

Jamison, Stephen. *Final Acts of Love: Families, Friends, and Assisted Dying.* New York, NY: Putnam, 1995.

Keown, John, Editor. *Euthanasia Examined: Ethical, Clinical, and Legal Perspectives.* New York, NY: Cambridge University Press, 1995.

Kessler, David. *The Rights of the Dying: A Companion for Life's Final Moments.* New York, NY: Harper Collins, 1997.

Kevorkian, Jack. *Prescription - Medicine: The Goodness of Planned Death.* Buffalo, NY: Prometheus Books, 1991.

Kogan, Barry S. *A Time to be Born and a Time to Die: The Ethics of Choice.* Hawthorne, NY: Aldine de Gruyter, 1991.

Koop, C. Everett. *The Right to Live: The Right to Die.* Wheaton, IL: Tyndale House Publishers, 1980.

Ladd, John, Editor. *Ethical Issues Relating to Life and Death.* New York, NY: Oxford University Press, 1979.

Larue, Gerald A. *Playing God: Fifty Religious Views on Your Right to Die.* Wakefield, RI: Moyer Bell, 1996.

Logue, Barbara. *Last Rights: Death Control and the Elderly in America.* New York, NY: Lexington Books, 1993.

Long, Robert E. *Suicide*. Bronx, NY: H.W. Wilson, 1995.

Lynn, Joanne, Editor. *By No Extraordinary Means: The Choice to Forego Life-Sustaining Food and Water*. Bloomington, IN: Indiana University Press, 1986.

Marcus, Eric. *Why Suicide? Answers to 200 of the Most Frequently Asked Questions about Suicide, Attempted Suicide, and Assisted Suicide*. San Francisco, CA: Harper, 1996.

Marker, Rita. *Deadly Compassion: The Death of Ann Humphry and the Truth About Euthanasia*. New York, NY: Wm. Morrow, 1993.

_____. *Euthanasia: Killing or Caring?* Lewiston, NY: Life Cycle Books, 1992.

McCaen, Gary E. *Doctor Assisted Suicide and the Euthanasia Movement*. Hudson, WI: G.E. McCaen Publications, 1994.

Meisel, Alan. *The Right to Die*. New York, NY: John Wiley & Sons, 1995.

Miskin, Robert I., Editor. *Euthanasia: The Good of the Patient, the Good of Society*. Frederick, MD: University Publishing Group, 1992.

Moreland, J.P., and Norman L. Geisler. *The Life and Death Debate: Moral Issues of Our Time*. Westport, CT: Greenwood Press, 1990.

Moreno, Jonathan D., Editor. *Arguing Euthanasia: The Controversy over Mercy Killing, Assisted Suicide and the "Right to Die."* New York, NY: Touchstone Books, 1995.

Munk, William. *Euthanasia: Or, Medical Treatment in Aid of an Easy Death*. Salem, NH: Ayer Co. Publishers, 1979.

New York State Task Force on Life and the Law Staff. *When Death is Sought: Assisted Suicide and Euthanasia in the Medical Context*. Albany, NY: New York State Task Force, 1994.

Nuland, Sherwin B. *How We Die: Reflections on Life's Final Chapter*. New York, NY: Alfred A. Knopf, 1994.

Overberg, Kenneth R., Editor. *Mercy or Murder? Euthanasia, Morality and Public Policy*. Kansas City, MO: Sheed & Ward, 1993.

The Physician and the Hopelessly Ill Patient: Legal, Medical, and Ethical Guidelines. New York, NY: Society for the Right to Die, 1985.

Quill, Timothy E. *Death and Dignity: Making Choices and Taking Charge*. New York, NY: W.W. Norton, 1993.

Quinlan, Joseph, and Julia Quinlan. *Karen Ann*. Garden City, NY: Doubleday & Co., 1977.

Rachels, James. *The End of Life: Euthanasia and Mortality*. New York, NY: Oxford University Press, 1986.

Riga, Peter J. *Right to Die or Right to Live? Legal Aspects of Dying and Death*. Gaithersburg, MD: Associated Faculty Press, 1981.

Rosenberg, Jay F. *Thinking Clearly About Death*. New York, NY: Prentice-Hall, 1983.

Rosenblatt, Stanley M. *Murder of Mercy: Euthanasia on Trial.* Buffalo, NY: Prometheus Books, 1992.

Russell, O. Ruth. *Freedom to Die: Moral and Legal Aspects of Euthanasia.* New York, NY: Human Sciences Press, 1977.

Shavelson, Lonny. *A Chosen Death: The Dying Confront Assisted Suicide.* New York, NY: Simon & Schuster, 1995.

Sherlock, Richard. *Preserving Life: Public Policy and the Life Not Worth Living.* Chicago, IL: Loyola Press, 1987.

Sloan, Irving J. *The Right to Die: Legal and Ethical Problems.* New York, NY: Oceana Publications, 1988.

Smith, Wesley J. *Forced Exit: The Slippery Slope from Assisted Suicide to Legalized Murder.* New York, NY: Times Books, 1997.

Steinbock, Bonnie, and Alastair Norcross, Editors. *Killing and Letting Die.* Bronx, NY: Fordham, 1994.

Tada, Joni E. *When Is It Right To Die? Suicide, Euthanasia, Suffering, Mercy.* Grand Rapids, MI: Zondervan Publishing House, 1992.

Thomasma, David C., and Glenn C. Graber. *Euthanasia: Toward an Ethical Social Policy.* New York, NY: Crossroad, 1990.

Urofsky, Melvin I. *Letting Go: Death, Dying, and the Law.* Norman, OK: University of Oklahoma Press, 1994.

Vaux, Kenneth L. *Death Ethics: Religious and Cultural Values in Prolonging and Ending Life.* Philadelphia, PA: Trinity Press International, 1992.

Wallace, Samuel E., and Albin Eser, Editors. *Suicide and Euthanasia: The Rights of Personhood.* Knoxville, TN: University of Tennessee Press, 1981.

Walter, James J., and Thomas A. Shannon, Editors. *Quality of Life: The New Medical Dilemma.* Mahwah, NJ: Paulist Press, 1990.

Weir, Robert F., Editor. *Physician-Assisted Suicide.* Bloomington, IN: Indiana University Press, 1997.

Wekesser, Carol, Editor. *Euthanasia: Opposing Viewpoints.* San Diego, CA: Greenhaven Press, 1995.

Wennberg, Robert N. *Terminal Choices: Euthanasia, Suicide, and the Right to Die.* Grand Rapids, MI: Wm. B. Eerdmans Publishing Co., 1990.

Westley, Dick. *When It's Right to Die: Conflicting Voices, Difficult Choices.* Mystic, CT: Twenty-Third Publications, 1995.

Wilson, Jerry B. *Death by Decision: The Medical, Moral, and Legal Dilemmas of Euthanasia.* Philadelphia, PA: Westminster Press, 1975.

Index

EXCELLENT BOOKS ORDER FORM

(Please xerox this form so it will be available to other readers.)

Please send
Copy(ies)

_____ of LIFE, DEATH, AND THE LAW @ $16.95
_____ of SCHOOLHOUSE DECISIONS @ $16.95
_____ of FREEDOM OF SPEECH DECISIONS @ $16.95
_____ of FREEDOM OF THE PRESS DECISIONS @ $16.95
_____ of FREEDOM OF RELIGION DECISIONS @ $16.95
_____ of THE MURDER REFERENCE @ $16.95
_____ of THE RAPE REFERENCE @ $16.95
_____ of LANDMARK DECISIONS @ $16.95
_____ of LANDMARK DECISIONS II @ $16.95
_____ of LANDMARK DECISIONS III @ $16.95
_____ of LANDMARK DECISIONS IV @ $16.95
_____ of LANDMARK DECISIONS V @ $16.95
_____ of ABORTION DECISIONS: THE 1970's @ $16.95
_____ of ABORTION DECISIONS: THE 1980's @ $16.95
_____ of ABORTION DECISIONS: THE 1990's @ $16.95
_____ of CIVIL RIGHTS DECISIONS: 19th CENTURY@ $16.95
_____ of CIVIL RIGHTS DECISIONS: 20th CENTURY @ $16.95
_____ of THE ADA HANDBOOK @ $16.95

Name: _____

Address: _____

City: _____ State: _____ Zip: _____

Add $1 per book for shipping and handling.
California residents add sales tax.

OUR GUARANTEE: Any Excellent Book may be returned at
any time for any reason and a full refund will be made.

Mail your check or money order to: Excellent Books,
Post Office Box 927105, San Diego, California 92192-7105
or call/fax (760) 598-5069